REGENTS CRITICS SERIES

General Editor: Paul A. Olson

LITERARY CRITICISM OF

GEORGE HENRY LEWES

The first five volumes of the Regents Critics Series, in addition
to the present volume, are:

Joseph Conrad on Fiction
Edited by Walter F. Wright

Critical Writings of Ford Madox Ford
Edited by Frank MacShane

Literary Criticism of Alexander Pope
Edited by Bertrand A. Goldgar

Literary Criticism of Edgar Allan Poe
Edited by Robert L. Hough

Literary Criticism of
George Henry Lewes

Edited by

ALICE R. KAMINSKY

UNIVERSITY OF NEBRASKA PRESS · LINCOLN

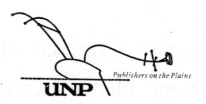

Copyright © 1964 by the University of Nebraska Press

Library of Congress Catalog card number 64–17230

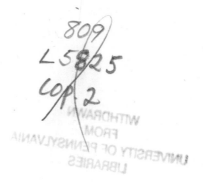

MANUFACTURED IN THE UNITED STATES OF AMERICA

Regents Critics Series

The Regents Critics Series provides reading texts of significant literary critics in the Western tradition. The series treats criticism as a useful tool: an introduction to the critic's own poetry and prose if he is a poet or novelist, an introduction to other work in his day if he is more judge than creator. Nowhere is criticism regarded as an end in itself but as what it is—a means to the understanding of the language of art as it has existed and been understood in various periods and societies.

Each volume includes a scholarly introduction which describes how the work collected came to be written, and suggests its uses. All texts are edited in the most conservative fashion consonant with the production of a good reading text; and all translated texts observe the dictum that the letter gives life and the spirit kills when a technical or rigorous passage is being put into English. Other types of passages may be more freely treated. Footnoting and other scholarly paraphernalia are restricted to the essential minimum. Such features as a bibliographical checklist or an index are carried where they are appropriate to the work in hand. If a volume is the first collection of the author's critical writing, this is noted in the bibliographical data.

PAUL A. OLSON

University of Nebraska

Contents

Introduction

Emily Dickinson once remarked that "Fame is a fickle food upon a shifting plate." When George Henry Lewes died, Matthew Arnold and other eminent Victorians predicted that his fame would endure. Yet curiously enough, one of the most remarkable men of the nineteenth century, esteemed as philosopher, scientist, and critic, is today more readily identified as the writer who lived with George Eliot. He deserved more. Even in an age which produced such figures as Carlyle, Ruskin, Arnold, and Mill, Lewes was a rare enough phenomenon, a thinker equally at ease in the fields of science and literature, viewing them not as antagonistic but as complementary fields of inquiry in a complex and changing universe.

The cause of science in the nineteenth century had no more devoted champion. As its advocate, he belongs with Darwin, Huxley, Mill, Spencer, Bain, Wundt, Taine, and Comte. In histories of philosophy, Lewes is usually categorized as one of the Comtist positivists, but this is a misleading classification. He wrote an explication of Comte's theories in 1853 (*Comte's Philosophy of the Sciences*); he never lost his admiration for certain Comtean principles. But he was too original a thinker to remain a mere disciple, and he lost Comte's friendship because he criticized his later mystical doctrines. No dogmatist for any cause, Lewes never tired of attacking absolutist theories. His belief in the efficacy of the scientific-empirical position grew more confirmed as he grew older. At the early age of twenty, he wrote: "We arrive then at the conclusion that we can never know but *relative* truth, our only medium of knowledge being the senses, and this medium, with regard *to all without us*, being forever a false one; but being *true to us*, we may put confidence in it relatively."[1] In one of his last volumes, *Foundations of a Creed*, he

[1] G. H. Lewes, "Hints towards an Essay on the Sufferings of Truth," *Monthly Repository*, II (1837), 314.

could still write: "Those who, affecting to despise the certainty attainable through Science, because it can never transcend the relative sphere, yearn for a knowledge which is not relative, and cheat themselves with phrases."[2] Lewes did not wish to be cheated; he remained a relativist to the last.

His antagonism toward the dogmatic biases of theological systems was so pronounced that he attempted to transform metaphysics into an empirical science, and he carried this antagonism into his literary criticism as well as his philosophic writing. His adverse comments on religion in the first volume of *Problems of Life and Mind* influenced John Blackwood to renege on his promise to publish it; Lewes' literary antipathy for the "religious world" is particularly evident in his remarks on Calderón and on the decline of the drama.[3] Like Pierce, Mead, and Dewey, he believed that the puzzles of existence could be solved without recourse to ontological or supranatural explanations. His analyses of scientific method, of verification, of real and ideal laws, of hypotheses, relativity, predictability, and causation are sound; and even if much of his more specific scientific speculation is dated, his general philosophic and scientific principles have become such an integral part of the modern empirical position as to be taken for granted. As a psychologist, Lewes belongs to the school of associationism which first came into prominence with the publication of Hartley's *Observations on Man* (1749) and which attained more complete development through the efforts of James Mill, John Stuart Mill, Herbert Spencer, and Alexander Bain. While much of Lewes' psychological terminology is outmoded, his attempt to apply the positive method to the study of mental phenomena is probably his most significant contribution. He insisted that scientific method in psychology requires an integration of the data of introspection, biology, and sociology. Although other writers, namely Comte and Spencer, had been

    [2] G. H. Lewes, *Foundations of a Creed* (2 vols.; London: H. Trübner, 1874, 1875), I, 201.
    [3] *The George Eliot Letters* (ed.), Gordon S. Haight (7 vols.; New Haven: Yale University Press, 1954–1956), V, 410; see pp. 135–137, 149–150 of this book.

impressed by the influence of social life upon mental life, Lewes
was the first to stress the special importance of the social factor
in psychological investigation, and to examine the extent and
nature of its influence. It is also to his credit that he developed
more fully than either Darwin or Spencer the psychological impli-
cations of biological evolution.

Since Lewes was a philosopher, we would expect his literary
theory to be related to his philosophic interests. He was a philosophic critic, but not in the traditional Hegelian sense, that is,
he did not examine all works of art in the light of an a priori,
metaphysical world view. He disliked those German critics who
tended to judge in terms of a *Weltanschauung* philosophy: he
disapproved of Augustus Schlegel whom he called a "synthetic"
critic, whereas he admired Lessing, the "analytic" critic. In his
critical as well as his philosophic writings, Lewes adhered to his
relativistic position. His articles on poetry and poets written in
the 1840's seem to ally him to the romantic-idealistic tradition in
criticism; his writings on the novel seem to place him in the
realist camp; and his dramatic criticism reflects a strong classical
influence. Small wonder then that his philosophy of art has been
variously characterized. It has been called classical, romantic,
Hegelian, realistic, sociological, psychoanalytic, and scientific.[4]
He wrote a great many articles, and it is possible to defend any
one of these points of view by concentrating on relevant portions
in certain essays and ignoring those which do not support the
particular thesis. Thus Lewes may appear to be a Hegelian in
his early years, since he wrote a long paper on Hegel's aesthetics
and even employed Hegelian terminology in a definition of
poetry; but he specifically stated that he did not accept Hegel's
ideas, and that he used Hegelian terminology in a positivistic

---

[4] Morris Greenhut, "George Henry Lewes and the Classical Tradition in
English Criticism," *Review of English Studies*, XXIV (1948), 126–137; Basil
Willey, *Nineteenth Century Studies* (New York: Columbia University Press,
1949), p. 245; H. A. Needham, *Le Développement de l'esthétique sociologique
en France et en Angleterre au xixe siècle* (Paris: Honoré Champion, 1926), p.
282; R. L. Brett, "George Henry Lewes: Dramatist, Novelist and Critic,"
Essays and Studies, XI (1958), 106–114.

sense. On the basis of a brief comment on the role of suffering in art in one of Lewes' articles, Basil Willey concluded that Lewes worked with a psychoneurotic theory of art. But none of these labels adequately characterizes his literary criticism. The variety of interpretations is induced primarily by Lewes' commitment to a critical relativism which is the logical correlative of his philosophic naturalism.

It may be well to define this critical relativism. First, to be a critical relativist for Lewes did not mean to be without tools for the analysis and judgment of art, but it did mean that different tools might be appropriate at different times. In the paper on Hegel, Lewes referred to the fundamental law of aesthetics as the "law of temporalities." This law denies that works of art can be judged *sub specie aeternitatis*. Furthermore, he objected to the use of traditional nomenclature—classic, romantic—since these terms had been hypostatized as if they signified some unchanging reality. He preferred to use the subjective-objective distinction which Schlegel, Schiller, and Browning had also employed, although he readily admitted that the terms *subjective* and *objective* were ambiguous. However, to him they did not connote value; instead they suggested kinds of psychological and cultural attitudes underlying works of art.

Second, Lewes viewed art as the result of an interaction between man and society. Art, like science and philosophy, is a means of enlarging man's understanding of himself and the universe: "We are forever seeing some new fact, some new quality, and again recombining it with others so as to bring together in a living synthesis objects that at first seemed wide as the poles asunder."[5] He was guided by the belief that art is the product of natural man in a natural world; it is not the divinely inspired revelation of the infinite. Art, like science and philosophy, cannot reveal eternal truths simply because they do not exist; for Lewes, only "truths of periods" exist. With Comte, he felt that art is essentially a social product. "Literature is . . . the *expres-*

---

[5] G. H. Lewes, *Mind as a Function of the Organism* (London: H. Trübner, 1879), pp. 493–494.

sion of society, which it in turn *reacts upon,* you cannot separate the two. . . . It stores up the accumulated experience of the race, connecting past and present into a conscious unity; and with this store it feeds successive generations, to be fed in turn by them."[6] As both the cause and effect of social progress, art serves the purpose of enlarging the sympathy and understanding of man. All of literature provides man with "the avenues through which we reach the sacred adytum of Humanity and learn better to understand our fellows and ourselves."[7] In short, art contributes to the improvement of society.

Third, ancient art does not constitute an artistic "rule of life." In *Foundations of a Creed,* Lewes wrote: "Not recognizing the social influence, men seldom appreciate the true point of view in discussions respecting ancient and modern Literature. It is undeniable that Sophocles, Plato, Aristotle, Hipparchus, and Galen were not less splendidly endowed than Shakespeare, Bacon, Newton, Comte, or Helmholtz—their intellectual lineaments may have been as grandly drawn, but it is absurd to pretend that the products of the ancient and the products of the modern mind are of anything like equal *value.*"[8] Lewes did have an admiration for the literary culture of the ancients. What he was inveighing against here was the servile idolizing of the classics, the mistaking of their historical significance for aesthetic significance. Since he believed that personal experience is the basis of all good art, he objected to the imitation of classical models; they were only to be used as valuable sources of enlightenment. As his discussion of Homer reveals, he had none of Matthew Arnold's donnish awe for the traditions of the past. He quoted with approval Schlegel's definition of the true critic: that man who has the flexibility and universality of mind which enables him to judge with sympathy

[6] G. H. Lewes, *The Life of Maximilien Robespierre* (London: Chapman, Hall, 1849), p. 21; "Principles of Success in Literature," *Fortnightly Review,* I (1865), 85.

[7] G. H. Lewes, "The Lady Novelists," *Westminster Review,* LVIII (1852), 130.

[8] G. H. Lewes, *Foundations of a Creed,* I, 174–175. See pp. 35–36 of this book.

and understanding the art of all nations and all periods, ancient and modern. Such a critic deplores absolutism of any kind and particularly avoids being confined by a conservatism which looks sentimentally to the past as the golden age of creativity.

Fourth, criticism depends upon the collection of evidence. In recent years, the opposition to critical relativism has been emphatically expressed by Cleanth Brooks who insists that "once we are committed to critical relativism, there can be no stopping short of a *complete* relativism in which critical judgments will disappear."[9] But surely this is to reduce sense to nonsense by ignoring the middle ground. Lewes' approach suggests that a middle ground is possible, that relativism does not have to degenerate into a meaningless subjectivism. Just as he had sought verification of hypotheses about the known world in his philosophic and scientific speculation, so he also sought corroboration of critical theories through the study of known artistic efforts: "To understand Nature, we must observe her manifestations, and trace out the laws of the coexistence of succession of phenomena. And, in the same way, to understand Art, we must patiently examine the works of art; and from a large observation of successful efforts, deduce general conclusions respecting the laws upon which success depends."[10] Since there can only be better or worse appraisals in the light of changes that are always occurring in man and society, Arnold's conception of a "real estimate" turns out, in this view, to be chimerical. Lewes regarded his empirical method as capable of enabling the artist, as well as the critic, to enlarge his understanding of the creative process. He saw it as giving the critic freedom to judge without being rigidly bound to certain dogmas; if, during his lifetime, the critic discovers that he has been wrong, he can change his mind to accommodate his individual judgments without embarrassing his theory. Thus, without being irrevocably committed to any one

[9] Cleanth Brooks, *The Well Wrought Urn: Studies in the Structure of Poetry* (New York: Harcourt, Brace, 1947), p. 234.

[10] G. H. Lewes, "Shakespeare's Critics: English and Foreign," *Edinburgh Review*, XC (1849), 68.

theory, and yet working with certain highly favored principles, Lewes was able to revise his opinion of Keats, Balzac, Charlotte Brontë, and Fielding.

Lewes originally believed that criticism could become a science through the empirical investigation of the procedures that have led to successful artistic efforts. He later recognized that criticism is an art which defies codification. His method was eclectic. In an essay on *Tom Jones*, he employs what we would call "judicial criticism." His study of Dickens is one of the earliest psychological analyses of the genius of this novelist. In "The Three Fausts," he relies upon comparative evaluation; in the Goethe biography he uses historical, biographical, and exegetical analysis. His writings on the drama reveal the eclectic method at its best, drawing as they do upon Aristotelian theory, upon Lessing's commentaries, and upon Romantic and neoclassic theories of the drama. Perhaps Lewes most resembles critics like I. A. Richards and Edmund Wilson who have emulated the Baconian ideal of wide learning and made use of philosophy, psychology, and sociology to obtain their insights. As Wilson turns from an examination of the Dead Sea Scrolls to Civil War Literature, so Lewes with equal facility turns from an excellent review of an opera, to the question of whether the Greek Chorus did or did not dance, to the problem of "Suicide in Life and Literature," and to a public affairs column in which he examines current events as a political liberal. He had what John Stuart Mill called a "buoyancy of spirit"[11] which made him attempt whatever interested him, and his interests ranged over the wide areas of Greek, Latin, Spanish, Italian, German, and American literature.

It should not be thought that Lewes, simply because he was a critical relativist, brought new light everywhere to criticism. What he had to say about the artist's function as a seer, the "laws" of literature, and the mechanics of style were Victorian commonplaces which Carlyle, Ruskin, and Spencer had also

---

[11] John Stuart Mill's letter to Macvey Napier (Feb. 18, 1842), British Museum Add. MSS. 34, 622.

stated. But he did bring to his analysis of the psychology of the artist's vision the "new light" of a novel and insightful point of view. The critics from Coleridge on were, in varying ways, involved with a transcendental view of reality. None of their theories grew out of scientific research; Lewes' theory of imagination evolved out of what he, as a physiological psychologist, had discovered about the workings of the mind. To those impressed by the Romantic theory of imagination, Lewes' analysis will seem prosaic, but modern aestheticians, born and bred in the scientific tradition, such as De Witt Parker, Stephen T. Pepper, John Dewey, and Irwin Edman, would approve of Lewes' approach.

Because Lewes did not see any warrant for distinguishing between creative and scientific vision as two opposite types of mental activity, he did not involve himself in the sort of fruitless controversy carried on by Shelley and Peacock, or Arnold and Huxley, which required choosing between Art and Science. Indeed, he was probably the only man in his period who had something sensible to say about the science-poetry antithesis dramatized by Coleridge and Wordsworth. Lewes maintained that the scientist and the artist employ the same kind of vision for different purposes and in different ways, and that imagination is no more the exclusive property of the artist than the cognitive faculty is the exclusive property of the scientist. Art, like science, has cognitive value, even though it is primarily concerned with feeling. It cannot afford to ignore the findings of science but must make use of them to enrich the substance of its creations. Even in his earliest criticism he singled out the superior poets by praising the philosophic content of their poems. Shelley, Goethe, and Shakespeare were concerned with ideas; Keats and the other Romantics, the Roman poets, and Wordsworth wrote poetry deficient in intellectual content. He praised George Eliot, Thackeray, Balzac, and George Sand for their deep concern with truth; he judged Dickens and Jane Austen, despite their skill, to be limited thinkers. He was an admirer of the art of acting and wrote one of the classic studies, *On Actors and the Art of Acting,* yet assigned the thespian the lowest status among the artists precisely because he believed that the actor is like a parasite who feeds upon the intellect of others without making any real intellectual contribution of his own.

Lewes felt that if art has cognitive value, if it is capable of enlarging the understanding of man, then those art works which most closely represent the real world are most likely to offer valuable insights. His conception of realism derives its justification from his belief in the cognitive value of art. Harold Osborne expressed the view of many modern aestheticians when he claimed that for purposes of critical exegesis, theories of realism have negligible meaning.[12] However, like the proverbial cat, they reappear. To understand what Lewes attempted to do with the theory of realism in literature, it is important to recall that he is applying in this connection the same monistic principle which characterizes his philosophy of "reasoned realism." Reasoned realism maintains that no dichotomy exists between what is mental and what is physical. Every experience presents a "double aspect": real and ideal, particular and general, subjective and objective. Regarded in one way, experience is subjective; regarded in another way, it is objective. For different purposes, experience is viewed differently, but the supposedly incompatible and separate material and mental operations are merely different aspects of the same process. Lewes carried this revolt against dualism into the field of art where he attempted to eliminate the distinction between realism and idealism. Idealism usually implies art which is nonexperiential as opposed to realism which implies art which is experiential or "true to nature," and therefore natural. But Lewes defined idealism as a higher type of realism which indicates that which is ideal in reality itself, and he opposed *falsism* to both realism and idealism. This critical monism, like his philosophical monism, is plagued by oversimplification and seems at times to be no more than a glib equivocation. But he applied the theory with particular effectiveness to combat

[12] Harold Osborne, *Aesthetics and Criticism* (New York: Philosophical Library, 1955), pp. 63–110.

what Proust derogated as "cinematographic realism."

The insistence that truth, not morality, is the prime criterion in judging the worth of any art product, led him to make some enlightened statements about the artist's obligation to deal with reality. In an excellent passage in *The Leader*, Lewes defended "nude statues and voluptuous verses"; his discussions of the novels of George Sand and Goethe's *Wilhelm Meister* and *Wahlverwandtschaften* reveal his essential lack of sympathy for the moralistic emphasis in criticism;[13] but he did not completely liberate himself from the "spirit of the age," and we find him worrying too much about the so-called immorality of the French novels, particularly those written by Balzac. What he advocated, after all, was a modified theory of realism. He believed that certain horrible realities are refractory to artistic treatment. It is safe to conjecture that he would have been repelled by a good many recent naturalistic novels.

In evaluating the great bulk of Lewes' literary criticism—books, articles, and reviews—we should be aware that his writing career was not a sideline but an economic necessity. He wrote some hack stuff, especially in the early years when he was trying to support a growing family. Remarkable as his review of *Moby Dick* is for its early recognition of the greatness of the novel, it contains little more than a pastiche of quotations from Melville's book. The dramatic criticism he wrote for *The Leader* illustrates both the advantages and disadvantages of being a reviewer forced to meet deadlines. His reviews reflect the enthusiasm with which he observed the plays as they were actually performed; they offer us invaluable, on-the-spot impressions of how plays were acted in mid-nineteenth century England; but they are deficient in the kind of theoretical analysis which appears in the more carefully prepared essays in which he examines the aesthetic presuppositions of dramatic art. Nor did he escape the pitfall of the journalist who must rely on his own taste to make new judgments. He overrated Elizabeth Barrett Browning and George Sand; he

---

[13] G. H. Lewes, *The Leader*, January 17, 1852, p. 60; "Balzac and George Sand," *Foreign Quarterly Review*, XXXIII (1844), 265–298; *The Life of Goethe* (3rd ed.; London: Smith, Elder, 1875), pp. 404–405, 512.

underrated Robert Browning, Balzac, and Keats. Anxious to encourage new writers, he overestimated the ability of some of the contemporary mediocre poets. We would expect inconsistencies to creep into the writings of a thinker whose period of productivity spanned more than forty years. He labeled Shakespeare a subjective artist in one article, and elsewhere referred to him as an objective artist.[14] But even in his most minor journalistic efforts, there is always evidence of perception, intelligence and wit. He never regarded the task of writing for the periodicals with the attitude of the bread scholar; he viewed periodical literature as an instrument for the education of the populace and the only means of making authorship a profession. He contributed to almost all of the important journals, and Carlyle justifiably called him the "Prince of Journalists." Lewes' earliest efforts were self-consciously learned, full of unnecessary references. But he gradually integrated his ideas into more effectively organized essays, of which the influential and controversial Dickens' criticism is one of the best examples. The writing defect which he himself characterized as "want of largo" he scrupulously tried to overcome by careful revision. Above all, he valued clarity. Although he considered De Quincey to be the greatest English prose stylist, he tried to avoid the eccentricities of an ornate and diffuse style.

He lived in an age when a desire to know everything was not yet a presumptuous madness, and when a man could, during one lifetime, be journalist, editor, critic, philosopher, psychologist, zoologist, biologist, actor, dramatist, novelist, and biographer. As Bulwer Lytton noted, Lewes had an "omnivorous intellectual appetite"; his versatility led Thackeray to observe that he would not be surprised to see Lewes riding down Piccadilly on a white elephant.[15] Objecting to specialization, Lewes himself defended

[14] G. H. Lewes in the *British and Foreign Review*, "Character and Works of Goethe," XIV (1843), 119; "Alfieri and the Italian Drama," XVII (1844), 369.

[15] Edward Robert Bulwer Lytton, 1st Earl of Lytton, *Personal and Literary Letters* ed. Lady Betty Balfour (2 vols.; London: Longmans, 1906), II, 137; H. Walker, *Literature of the Victorian Era* (Cambridge: Cambridge University Press, 1910), p. 179.

the versatile writer: "The public like a man to confine himself to one special topic. Division of labour is the grand thing: if you have made pins' heads, content yourself with that, and do not venture upon points. Accordingly we see men always working the mine where they once discovered gold, and afraid to dig elsewhere. They repeat themselves."[16] His interests gave him a vantage point from which to judge enjoyed by few critics of the century. Worldly in outlook, lacking the provincialism of the insular Englishman, he was fair and undogmatic. Anticipating Matthew Arnold in his attempt to make the critic a respected professional, he condemned the errors and abuses of English criticism.[17] He particularly despised that criticism which ignores the sensitivities of others, and broke off his friendship with Robert W. Buchanan because of Buchanan's anonymous attack on Rossetti in "The Fleshly School of Poetry."[18] Although his tastes were generally catholic—his list of the greatest poets includes Homer, Sophocles, Dante, Shakespeare, Milton, and Goethe—he refused to accept opinions simply because they had the sanction of time and great men.

The most just praise he received came from G. J. Holyoake: "Lewes was intellectually the bravest man I have known. . . . When he accepted a principle, he accepted all that belongs to it. Courage means facing a danger by force of will, facing danger which you know to be such. Men of natural intrepidity never take danger into account or, if they are conscious of it, it only influences them as an inspiration to action. Mr. Lewes had intellectual intrepidity of this kind."[19] In his philosophical as well as in his critical speculation, Lewes played the role of gadfly, questioning traditional beliefs and, in true maverick fashion, daring to assail even the unassailable Homer and Shakespeare. He de-

---

[16] G. H. Lewes, "Memoir of Sir E. Bulwer Lytton, Bart.," *Bentley's Magazine,* XXIV (1848), 9.

[17] G. H. Lewes, "The Errors and Abuses of English Criticism," *Westminster Review,* XXXVIII (1842), 466–486.

[18] *The George Eliot Letters,* VII, 89.

[19] G. J. Holyoake, *Sixty Years of an Agitator's Life* (2 vols.: London: T. Fisher Unwin, 1892), I, 243.

serves to be recognized, to use George Bernard Shaw's words, "as the most able and brilliant critic" between Hazlitt and Arnold.[20]

Note on the Text

All the articles included in this volume are reprinted from the magazines in which they originally appeared, except those on acting which Lewes himself edited for his book *On Actors and the Art of Acting.* A few minor alterations have been introduced to eliminate inconsistencies in spelling and punctuation. Some quotations which originally appeared in the text in a language other than English have been translated by the editor; in such cases the quotation is given in its original form in a footnote. A bibliographical note appears at the end of each selection. The essays have been selected and arranged to illustrate the significant emphases of Lewes' criticism. In the first two sections he discusses general theories: scientific and artistic perception and cognition, and the relationship between the changing conventions of human cultures and the "style" and "truth" of the art produced by those cultures. The application of literary principles is to be found in the last four sections where he criticizes individual poets, novelists, actors, and dramatists.

ALICE R. KAMINSKY

State University of New York, College at Cortland, New York

[20] George Bernard Shaw, *The Collected Works* (30 vols.; New York: W. H. Wise, 1931), XXV, 163. The quotation from Shaw reads, "The most able and brilliant critic between Hazlitt and our own contemporaries."

Biographical Note

George Henry Lewes was born in London on April 18, 1817, the youngest of three sons of John Lee and Elizabeth Ashweek Lewes. He attended various schools, including Dr. Charles Parr Burney's famous institution at Greenwich. When he left Greenwich in 1833, he drifted from one clerical position to another, preoccupying himself even in those early years with the study of medicine and science. He was employed as a tutor in Germany in 1838 and 1840. On February 18, 1841, he married Agnes Swynfen Jervis (1822–1902) who bore him four sons. Without influential family or a university career to aid him, Lewes was able through tireless intellectual activity to earn for himself an enviable reputation in the literary world. His first book, *The Biographical History of Philosophy* (1845), proved to be very popular. He published a commentary on the Spanish drama in 1846; *Ranthorpe,* a novel, in 1847; another novel, *Rose, Blanche, and Violet,* in 1848; and the first English biography of Robespierre in 1849. In 1850 he became editor of *The Leader,* a liberal weekly, and among his many contributions to it were a series of articles on Comte, later published in 1853 as *Comte's Philosophy of the Sciences.* By 1854 Lewes had separated from his wife who had committed adultery with Thorton Hunt, and on July 20 of that year Lewes left for Germany in the company of George Eliot. This departure signaled the beginning of Lewes' life with the great novelist, an association that was to bring them both many years of rewarding happiness. In 1855 Lewes published his famous biography of Goethe, but from 1856 scientific research absorbed his time as a dominant interest. *Sea-Side Studies at Ilfracombe, Tenby, the Scilly Isles and Jersey* appeared in 1858, followed by *The Physiology of Common Life* (1859), *Studies in Animal Life* (1862), and *Aristotle: A Chapter in the History of Science* (1864). Lewes edited the *Fortnightly Review* from 1865 to 1866, contributing scientific, political, and literary material. The later years of his life were saddened by the early deaths of two of his sons and by recurring periods of ill health. On November 30, 1878, he died of enteritis, leaving to George Eliot the task of editing the last few volumes of his five-volume work on philosophy and science, *Problems of Life and Mind* (1874–1879).

I.

ON COGNITION: ART AND SCIENCE

In the following selections, three asterisks (* * *) indicate that a portion of the original has been omitted.

Mental Vision

Insight is the first condition of Art. Yet many a man who has never been beyond his village will be silent about that which he knows well, and will fancy himself called upon to speak of the tropics or the Andes—on the reports of others. Never having seen a greater man than the parson and the squire—and not having seen into them—he selects Cromwell and Plato, Raphael and Napoleon, as his models, in the vain belief that these impressive personalities will make his work impressive. Of course I am speaking figuratively. By "never having been beyond his village," I understand a mental no less than topographical limitation. The penetrating sympathy of genius will, even from a village, traverse the whole world. What I mean is, that unless by personal experience, no matter through what avenues, a man has gained clear insight into the facts of life, he cannot successfully place them before us; and whatever insight he *has* gained, be it of important or of unimportant facts, will be of value if truly reproduced. No sunset is precisely similar to another, no two souls are affected by it in a precisely similar way. Thus may the commonest phenomenon have a novelty. To the eye that can read aright there is an infinite variety even in the most ordinary human being. But to the careless indiscriminating eye all individuality is merged in a misty generality. Nature and men yield nothing new to such a mind. Of what avail is it for a man to walk out into the tremulous mists of morning, to watch the slow sunset, and wait for the rising stars, if he can tell us nothing about these but what others have already told us—if he feels nothing but what others have already felt? Let a man look for himself and tell truly what he sees. We will listen to that. We must listen to it, for its very authenticity has a subtle power of compulsion. What others have seen and felt we can learn better from their own lips.

I have not yet explained in any formal manner what the

nature of that insight is which constitutes what I have named the Principle of Vision; although doubtless the reader has gathered its meaning from the remarks already made. For the sake of future applications of the principle to the various questions of philosophical criticism which must arise in the course of this inquiry, it may be needful here to explain (as I have already explained elsewhere)[1] how the chief intellectual operations—Perception, Inference, Reasoning, and Imagination—may be viewed as so many forms of mental vision.

Perception, as distinguished from Sensation, is the presentation before Consciousness of the details which once were present in conjunction with the object at this moment affecting Sense. These details are inferred to be still in conjunction with the object, although not revealed to Sense. Thus when an apple is perceived by me, who merely see it, all that Sense reports is of a certain coloured surface: the roundness, the firmness, the fragrance, and the taste of the apple are not present to Sense, but are made present to Consciousness by the act of Perception. The eye sees a certain coloured surface; the mind sees at the same instant many other co-existent but unapparent facts—it reinstates in their due order these unapparent facts. Were it not for this mental vision supplying the deficiencies of ocular vision, the coloured surface would be an enigma. But the suggestion of Sense rapidly recalls the experiences previously associated with the object. The apparent facts disclose the facts that are unapparent.

Inference is only a higher form of the same process. We look from the window, see the dripping leaves and the wet ground, and infer that rain has fallen. It is on inferences of this kind that all knowledge depends. The extension of the known to the unknown, of the apparent to the unapparent, gives us Science. Except in the grandeur of its sweep, the mind pursues the same course in the interpretation of geological facts as in the interpretation of the ordinary incidents of daily experience. To read the

---

[1] G. H. Lewes, *The Biographical History of Philosophy* (London: John W. Parker, 1857), pp. xxviii–xxix.

pages of the great Stone Book, and to perceive from the wet streets that rain has recently fallen, are forms of the same intellectual process. In the one case the inference traverses immeasurable spaces of time, connecting the apparent facts with causes (unapparent facts) similar to those which have been associated in experience with such results; in the other case the inference connects wet streets and swollen gutters with causes which have been associated in experience with such results. Let the inference span with its mighty arch a myriad of years, or link together the events of a few minutes, in each case the arch rises from the ground of familiar facts, and reaches an antecedent which is known to be a cause capable of producing them.

The mental vision by which in Perception we see the unapparent details—*i.e.* by which sensations formerly co-existing with the one now affecting us are reinstated under the form of ideas which *represent* the objects—is a process implied in all Ratiocination, which also presents an *ideal series,* such as would be a series of sensations, if the objects themselves were before us. A chain of reasoning is a chain of inferences: *ideal* presentations of objects and relations not apparent to Sense, or not presentable to Sense. Could we realize all the links in this chain, by placing the objects in their actual order as a *visible* series, the reasoning would be a succession of perceptions. Thus the path of a planet is seen by reason to be an ellipse. It would be perceived as a fact, if we were in a proper position and endowed with the requisite means of following the planet in its course; but not having this power, we are reduced to infer the unapparent points in its course from the points which are apparent. We see them mentally. Correct reasoning is the ideal assemblage of objects in their actual order of co-existence and succession. It is seeing with the mind's eye. False reasoning is owing to some misplacement of the order of objects, or to the omission of some links in the chain, or to the introduction of objects not properly belonging to the series. It is distorted or defective vision. The terrified traveller sees a highwayman in what is really a sign-post in the twilight; and in the twilight of knowledge, the terrified philosopher sees a pestilence foreshadowed by an eclipse.

Let attention also be called to one great source of error, which is also a great source of power, namely, that much of our thinking is carried on by signs instead of images. We use words as signs of objects; these suffice to carry on the train of inference, when very few images of the objects are called up. Let any one attend to his thoughts and he will be surprised to find how rare and indistinct in general are the images of objects which arise before his mind. If he says "I shall take a cab and get to the railway by the shortest cut," it is ten to one that he forms no image of cab or railway, and but a very vague image of the streets through which the shortest cut will lead. Imaginative minds see images where ordinary minds see nothing but signs: this is a source of power; but it is also a source of weakness; for in the practical affairs of life, and in the theoretical investigations of philosophy, a too active imagination is apt to distract the attention and scatter the energies of the mind.

In complex trains of thought signs are indispensable. The images, when called up, are only vanishing suggestions: they disappear before they are more than half formed. And yet it is because signs are thus substituted for images (paper transacting the business of money) that we are so easily imposed upon by verbal fallacies and meaningless phrases. A scientific man of some eminence was once taken in by a wag, who gravely asked him whether he had read Bunsen's paper on the *malleability* of light. He confessed that he had not read it: "Bunsen sent it to me, but I've not had time to look into it."

The degree in which each mind habitually substitutes signs for images will be, *ceteris paribus*, the degree in which it is liable to error. This is not contradicted by the fact that mathematical, astronomical, and physical reasonings may, when complex, be carried on more successfully by the employment of signs; because in these cases the signs themselves accurately represent the abstractness of the relations. Such sciences deal only with relations, and not with objects; hence greater simplification ensures greater accuracy. But no sooner do we quit this sphere of abstractions to enter that of concrete things, than the use of symbols becomes a source of weakness. Vigorous and effective minds habitually deal with concrete images. This is notably the case with poets and great literates. Their vision is keener than that of other men. However rapid and remote their flight of thought, it is a succession of images, not of abstractions. The details which give significance, and which by us are seen vaguely as through a vanishing mist, are by them seen in sharp outlines. The image which to us is a mere suggestion, is to them almost as vivid as the object. And it is because they see vividly that they can paint effectively.

Most readers will recognize this to be true of poets, but will doubt its application to philosophers, because imperfect psychology and unscientific criticism have disguised the identity of intellectual processes until it has become a paradox to say that imagination is not less indispensable to the philosopher than to the poet. The paradox falls directly we restate the proposition thus: both poet and philosopher draw their power from the energy of their mental vision—an energy which disengages the mind from the somnolence of habit and from the pressure of obtrusive sensations. In general men are passive under Sense and the routine of habitual inferences. They are unable to free themselves from the importunities of the apparent facts and apparent relations which solicit their attention; and when they make room for unapparent facts it is only for those which are familiar to their minds. Hence they can see little more than what they have been taught to see; they can only think what they have been taught to think. For independent vision, and original conception, we must go to children and men of genius. The spontaneity of the one is the power of the other. Ordinary men live among marvels and feel no wonder, grow familiar with objects and learn nothing new about them. Then comes an independent mind which *sees*; and it surprises us to find how servile we have been to habit and opinion, how blind to what we also might have seen, had we used our eyes. The link, so long hidden, has now been made visible to us. We hasten to make it visible to others. But the flash of light which revealed that obscured object does not help us to discover others. Darkness still conceals much that we do not even suspect. We continue our routine. We always think our views correct and complete; if we thought otherwise they would cease to be our views; and when the man of keener insight discloses our error, and reveals relations hitherto unsuspected, we learn to see with his eyes and exclaim: "Now surely we have got the truth."

A child is playing with a piece of paper and brings it near the flame of a candle; another child looks on. Both are completely absorbed by the objects, both are ignorant or oblivious of the relation between the combustible object and the flame: a relation which becomes apparent only when the paper is alight. What is called the thoughtlessness of childhood prevents their seeing this unapparent fact; it is a fact which has not been sufficiently impressed upon their experience so as to form an indissoluble element in their conception of the two in juxtaposition. Whereas in the mind of the nurse this relation is so vividly impressed that no sooner does the paper approach the flame than the unapparent fact becomes almost as visible as the objects, and a warning is given. She sees what the children do not, or cannot see. It has become part of her organized experience.

The superiority of one mind over another depends on the rapidity with which experiences are thus organized. The superiority may be general or special: it may manifest itself in a power of assimilating very various experiences, so as to have manifold relations familiar to it, or in a power of assimilating very special relations, so as to constitute a distinctive aptitude for one branch of art or science. The experience which is thus organized must of course have been originally a direct object of consciousness, either as an impressive fact or impressive inference. Unless the paper had been seen to burn, no one could know that contact with flame would consume it. By a vivid remembrance the experience of the past is made available to the present, so that we do not need actually to burn paper once more,—we see the relation mentally. In like manner Newton did not need to go through the demonstrations of many complex problems, they flashed upon him as he read the propositions; they were seen by him in that rapid glance, as they would have been made visible through the slower process of demonstration. A good chemist does not need to test many a proposition by bringing actual gases or acids into operation, and seeing the result; he *foresees* the result: his mental vision of the objects and their properties is so keen, his experience is so organized, that the result which would be visible in an experiment, is visible to him in an intuition. A fine poet has no need of the actual presence of men and women under the fluctuating impatience of emotion, or under the steadfast hopelessness of grief; he needs no setting sun before his window, under it no sullen sea. These are all visible, and their fluctuations are visible. He sees the quivering lip, the agitated soul; he hears the aching cry, and the dreary wash of waves upon the beach.

The writer who pretends to instruct us should first assure himself that he has clearer vision of the things he speaks of,— knows them and their qualities, if not better than we, at least with some distinctive knowledge. Otherwise he should announce himself as a mere echo, a middleman, a distributor. Our need is for more light. This can be given only by an independent seer who

Lends a precious seeing to the eye. * * *[2]

"Principles of Success in Literature," *Fortnightly Review*, I (1865), 182–192. T. Sharper Knowlson and F. N. Scott have published editions of this work; see bibliography.

[2] "It adds a precious seeing to the eye." *Love's Labour Lost*, **IV**, iii.

Of Vision in Art: The Nature of the Imagination

There are many who will admit, without hesitation, that in Philosophy what I have called the Principle of Vision holds an important rank, because the mind must necessarily err in its speculations unless it clearly sees fact and relations; but there are some who will hesitate before admitting the principle to a similar rank in Art, because, as they conceive, Art is independent of the truth of facts, and is swayed by the autocratic power of Imagination.

It is on this power that our attention should first be arrested; the more so because it is usually spoken of in vague rhapsodical language, with intimations of its being something peculiarly mysterious. There are few words more abused. The artist is called a creator, which in one sense he is; and his creations are said to be produced by processes wholly unallied to the creations of Philosophy, which they are not. Hence it is a paradox to speak of the *Principia* as a creation demanding severe and continuous exercise of the imagination; but it is only a paradox to those who have never analyzed the processes of artistic and philosophic creation. * * *

There is, for instance, a broad distinction between Science and Art, which, so far from requiring to be effaced, requires to be emphasized: it is that in Science the paramount appeal is to the Intellect—its purpose being instruction; in Art, the paramount appeal is to the Emotions—its purpose being pleasure. A work of Art must of course indirectly appeal to the Intellect, and a work of Science will also indirectly appeal to the Feelings; nevertheless a poem on the stars and a treatise on astronomy have distinct aims and distinct methods. But having recognized the broadly-marked differences, we are called upon to ascertain the underlying resemblances. Logic and Imagination belong equally to both. It is only because men have been attracted by the differences that they have overlooked the not less important affinities.

10

Imagination is an intellectual process common to Philosophy and Art; but in each it is allied with different processes, and directed to different ends; and hence, although the *Principia* demanded an imagination of not less vivid and sustained power than was demanded by *Othello*, it would be very false psychology to infer that the mind of Newton was competent to the creation of *Othello*, or the mind of Shakespeare capable of producing the *Principia*. They were specifically different minds; their works were specifically different. But in both the imagination was intensely active. Newton had a mind predominantly ratiocinative: its movement was spontaneously towards the abstract relations of things. Shakespeare had a mind predominantly emotive, the intellect always moving in alliance with the feelings, and spontaneously fastening upon the concrete facts in preference to their abstract relations. Their mental Vision was turned towards images of different orders, and it moved in alliance with different faculties; but this Vision was the cardinal quality of both. Dr. Johnson was guilty of a surprising fallacy in saying that a great mathematician might also be a great poet: "Sir, a man can walk east as far as he can walk west."[1] True, but mathematics and poetry do not differ as east and west; and he would hardly assert that a man who could walk twenty miles could therefore swim that distance.

The real state of the case is somewhat obscured by our observing that many men of science, and some even eminent as teachers and reporters, display but slender claims to any unusual vigour of imagination. It must be owned that they are often slightly dull; and in matters of Art are not unfrequently blockheads. Nay, they would themselves repel it as a slight if the epithet "imaginative" were applied to them; it would seem to impugn their gravity, to cast doubts upon their accuracy. But such men are the cisterns, not the fountains, of Science. They rely upon the knowledge already organized; they do not bring accessions to the com-

---

[1] "Sir, the man who has vigour may walk to the east, just as well as to the west, if he happens to turn his head that way." *Boswell's Journal of a Tour to the Hebrides with Samuel Johnson LL.D.*, edd. F. A. Pottle and C. A. Bennett (Yale Edition; New York: McGraw Hill, 1961), p. 20.

mon stock. They are not investigators, but imitators; they are not discoverers—inventors. No man ever made a discovery (he may have stumbled on one) without the exercise of as much imagination as, employed in another direction and in alliance with other faculties, would have gone to the creation of a poem. Every one who has seriously investigated a novel question, who has really interrogated Nature with a view to a distinct answer, will bear me out in saying that it requires intense and sustained effort of imagination. The relations of sequence among the phenomena must be seen; they are hidden; they can only be seen mentally; a thousand suggestions rise before the mind, but they are recognized as old suggestions, or as inadequate to reveal what is sought; the experiments by which the problem may be solved have to be imagined; and to imagine a good experiment is as difficult as to invent a good fable, for we must have distinctly *present*—in clear mental vision—the known qualities and relations of all the objects, and must *see* what will be the effect of introducing some new qualifying agent. If any one thinks this is easy, let him try it: the trial will teach him a lesson respecting the methods of intellectual activity not without its use. Easy enough, indeed, is the ordinary practice of experiment, which is either a mere repetition or variation of experiments already devised (as ordinary story-tellers re-tell the stories of others), or else a haphazard, blundering way of bringing phenomena together, to see what will happen. To invent is another process. The discoverer and the poet are inventors; and they are so because their mental vision detects the unapparent, unsuspected facts, almost as vividly as ocular vision rests on the apparent and familiar.

It is the special aim of Philosophy to discover and systematize the abstract *relations* of things; and for this purpose it is forced to allow the things themselves to drop out of sight, fixing attention solely on the quality immediately investigated, to the neglect of all other qualities. Thus the philosopher, having to appreciate the mass, density, refracting power, or chemical constitution of some object, finds he can best appreciate this by isolating it from every other detail. He abstracts this one quality from the complex bundle of qualities which constitute the object, and he makes this one stand for the whole. This is a necessary simplification. If all the qualities were equally present to his mind, his vision would be perplexed by their multiple suggestions. He may follow out the relations of each in turn, but he cannot follow them out together.

The aim of the poet is very different. He wishes to kindle the emotions by the suggestion of objects themselves; and for this purpose he must present images of the objects rather than of any single quality. It is true that he also must exercise a power of abstraction and selection. He cannot without confusion present all the details. And it is here that the fine selective instinct of the true artist shows itself, in knowing what details to present and what to omit. Observe this: the abstraction of the philosopher is meant to keep the object itself, with its perturbing suggestions, out of sight, allowing only one quality to fill the field of vision; whereas the abstraction of the poet is meant to bring the object itself into more vivid relief, to make it visible by means of the selected qualities. In other words, the one aims at abstract symbols, the other at picturesque effects. The one can carry on his deductions by the aid of colourless signs, x or y. The other appeals to the emotions through the symbols which will most vividly express the real objects in their relations to our sensibilities.

Imagination is obviously active in both. From known facts the philosopher infers the facts that are unapparent. He does so by an effort of imagination (hypothesis) which has to be subjected to verification: he makes a mental picture of the unapparent fact, and then sets about to prove that his picture does in some way correspond with the reality. The correctness of his hypothesis and verification must depend on the clearness of his vision. Were all the qualities of things apparent to Sense, there would be no longer any mystery. A glance would be Science. But only some of the facts are visible; and it is because we see little, that we have to imagine much. We see a feather rising in the air, and a quill, from the same bird, sinking to the ground: these contradictory reports of sense lead the mind astray; or perhaps excite a desire to know the reason. We cannot see—we must imagine—the unapparent facts. Many mental pictures may be formed, but to form the one which corresponds with the reality requires great sagacity and a very clear vision of known facts. In trying to form this mental picture we remember that when the air is removed the feather falls as rapidly as the quill, and thus we *see* that the air is the cause of the feather's rising; we mentally see the air pushing under the feather, and see it almost as plainly as if the air were a visible mass thrusting the feather upwards.

From a mistaken appreciation of the real process this would by few be called an effort of Imagination. On the contrary some "wild hypothesis" would be lauded as imaginative in proportion as it departed from all suggestion of experience, *i.e.* real mental vision. To have imagined that the feather rose owing to its "specific lightness," and that the quill fell owing to its "heaviness," would to many appear a more decided effort of the imaginative faculty. Whereas it is no effort of that faculty at all; it is simply naming differently the facts it pretends to explain. To imagine— to form an image—we must have the numerous relations of things present to the mind, and see the objects in their actual order. In this we are of course greatly aided by the mass of organized experience, which allows us rapidly to estimate the relations of gravity or affinity just as we remember that fire burns and that heated bodies expand. But be the aid great or small, and the result victorious or disastrous, the imaginative process is always the same.

There is a slighter strain on the imagination of the poet, because of his greater freedom. He is not, like the philosopher, limited to the things which are, or were. His vision includes things which might be, and things which never were. The philosopher is not entitled to assume that Nature sympathizes with man; he must prove the fact to be so if he intend making any use of it;—we admit no deductions from unproved assumptions. But the poet is at perfect liberty to assume this; and having done so, he paints what would be the manifestations of this sympathy. The naturalist who should describe a hippogriff would incur the laughing scorn of Europe; but the poet feigns its existence, and all Europe is delighted when it rises with Astolfo in the air. We never pause to ask the poet whether such an animal exists. He has seen it, and we see it with his eyes. Talking trees do not startle us in Virgil and Tennyson. Puck and Titania, Hamlet and Falstaff, are as true for us as Luther and Napoleon, so long as we are in the realm of Art. We grant the poet a free privilege because he will use it only for our pleasure. In Science pleasure is not an object, and we give no licence.

Philosophy and Art both render the invisible visible by imagination. Where Sense observes two isolated objects, Imagination discloses two related objects. This relation is the nexus visible. We had not seen it before; it is apparent now. Where we should only see a calamity the poet makes us see a tragedy. * * *

Imagination is not the exclusive appanage of artists, but belongs in varying degrees to all men. It is simply the power of forming images. Supplying the energy of Sense where Sense cannot reach, it brings into distinctness the facts, obscure or occult, which are grouped round an object or an idea, but which are not actually present to Sense. Thus, at the aspect of a windmill, the mind forms images of many characteristic facts relating to it; and the kind of images will depend very much on the general disposition, or particular mood, of the mind affected by the object: the painter, the poet, and the moralist will have different images suggested by the presence of the windmill or its symbol. There are indeed sluggish minds so incapable of self-evolved activity, and so dependent on the immediate suggestions of Sense, as to be almost destitute of the power of forming distinct images beyond the immediate circle of sensuous associations; and these are rightly named unimaginative minds; but in all minds of energetic activity, groups and clusters of images, many of them representing remote relations, spontaneously present themselves in conjunction with objects or their symbols. It should, however, be borne in mind that Imagination can only recall what Sense has previously impressed. No man imagines any detail of which he has not previously had direct or indirect experience. Objects as fictitious as mermaids and hippogriffs are made up from the gatherings of Sense.

"Made up from the gatherings of Sense" is a phrase which may seem to imply some peculiar plastic power such as is claimed exclusively for artists: a power not of simple recollection, but of recollection and recombination. Yet this power belongs also to philosophers. To combine the half of a woman with the half of a fish,—to imagine the union as an existing organism,—is not really a different process from that of combining the experience of a chemical action with an electric action, and seeing that the two are one existing fact. When the poet hears the storm-cloud muttering, and sees the moonlight sleeping on the bank, he transfers his experience of human phenomena to the cloud and the moonlight: he personifies, draws Nature within the circle of emotion, and is called a poet. When the philosopher sees electricity in the storm-cloud, and sees the sunlight stimulating vegetable growth, he transfers his experience of physical phenomena to these objects, and draws within the circle of Law phenomena which hitherto have been unclassified. Obviously the imagination has been as active in the one case as in the other; the *differentia* lying in the purposes of the two, and in the general constitution of the two minds.

It has been noted that there is less strain on the imagination of the poet; but even his greater freedom is not altogether disengaged from the necessity of verification; his images must have at least subjective truth; if they do not accurately correspond with objective realities, they must correspond with our sense of congruity. No poet is allowed the licence of creating images inconsistent with our conceptions. If he said the moonlight *burnt* the bank, we should reject the image as untrue, inconsistent with our conceptions of moonlight; whereas the gentle repose of the moonlight on the bank readily associates itself with images of sleep.

The often mooted question, What is Imagination? thus receives a very clear and definite answer. It is the power of forming images; it reinstates, in a visible group, those objects which are invisible, either from absence or from imperfection of our senses. That is its generic character. Its specific character, which marks it off from Memory, and which is derived from the powers of selection and recombination, will be expounded further on. Here I only touch upon its chief characteristic, in order to disengage the term from that mysteriousness which writers have usually assigned to it, thereby rendering philosophic criticism impossible. Thus disengaged it may be used with more certainty in an attempt to estimate the imaginative power of various works.

Hitherto the amount of that power has been too frequently estimated according to the extent of *departure* from ordinary experience in the images selected. Nineteen out of twenty would unhesitatingly declare that a hippogriff was a greater effort of imagination than a well-conceived human character; a Peri than a woman; Puck or Titania than Falstaff or Imogen. A description of Paradise extremely unlike any known garden must, it is thought, necessarily be more imaginative than the description of a quiet rural nook. It may be more imaginative; it may be less so. All depends upon the mind of the poet. To suppose that it must, because of its departure from ordinary experience, is a serious error. The muscular effort required to draw a cheque for a thousand pounds might as reasonably be thought greater than that required for a cheque of five pounds; and much as the one cheque seems to surpass the other in value, the result of presenting both to the bankers may show that the more modest cheque is worth its full five pounds, whereas the other is only so much waste paper. The description of Paradise may be a glittering farrago; the description of the landscape may be full of sweet rural images: the one having a glare of gaslight and Vauxhall splendour; the other having the scent of new-mown hay.

A work is imaginative in virtue of the power of its images over our emotions; not in virtue of any rarity or surprisingness in the images themselves. A Madonna and Child by Fra Angelico is more powerful over our emotions than a Crucifixion by a vulgar artist; a beggar-boy by Murillo is more imaginative than an Assumption by the same painter; but the Assumption by Titian displays far greater imagination than either. We must guard against the natural tendency to attribute to the artist what is entirely due to accidental conditions. A tropical scene, luxuriant with tangled overgrowth and impressive in the grandeur of its phenomena, may more decisively arrest our attention than an English landscape with its green corn lands and plenteous homesteads. But this superiority of interest is no proof of the artist's

superior imagination; and by a spectator familiar with the tropics, greater interest may be felt in the English landscape, because
its images may more forcibly arrest his attention by their novelty.
And were this not so, were the inalienable impressiveness of tropical scenery always to give the poet who described it a superiority
in effect, this would not prove the superiority of his imagination.
For either he has been familiar with such scenes, and imagines
them just as the other poet imagines his English landscape—by
an effort of mental vision, calling up the absent objects; or he has
merely read the descriptions of others, and from these makes up
his picture. It is the same with his rival, who also recalls and
recombines. Foolish critics often betray their ignorance by saying
that a painter or a writer "only copies what he has seen, or puts
down what he has known." They forget that no man imagines
what he has not seen or known, and that it is in the *selection of
the characteristic details* that the artistic power is manifested.
Those who suppose that familiarity with scenes or characters
enables a painter or a novelist to "copy" them with artistic effect,
forget the well-known fact that the vast majority of men are painfully incompetent to avail themselves of this familiarity, and
cannot form vivid pictures even to themselves of scenes in which
they pass their daily lives; and if they could imagine these, they
would need the delicate selective instinct to guide them in the
admission and omission of details, as well as in the grouping of
the images. * * *

It has been well said by a very imaginative writer, that "when
a poet floats in the empyrean, and only takes a bird's-eye view of
the earth, some people accept the mere fact of his soaring for
sublimity, and mistake his dim vision of earth for proximity to
heaven."[2] And in like manner, when a thinker frees himself from
all the trammels of fact, and propounds a "bold hypothesis," people mistake the vagabond erratic flights of guessing for a higher
range of philosophic power. In truth, the imagination is most
tasked when it has to paint pictures which shall withstand the

---

[2] George Eliot, "Worldliness and Other-Worldliness: The Poet Young,"
Westminster Review, LXVII (1857), 27.

silent criticism of general experience and to frame hypotheses which shall withstand the confrontation with facts. * * * I wish to call special attention to the psychological fact, that fairies and demons, remote as they are from experience, are not created by a more vigorous effort of imagination than milkmaids and poachers. The intensity of vision in the artist and of vividness in his creations are the sole tests of his imaginative power. * * *

By reducing imagination to the power of forming images, and by insisting that no image can be formed except out of the elements furnished by experience, I do not mean to confound imagination with memory; indeed, the frequent occurrence of great strength of memory with comparative feebleness of imagination, would suffice to warn us against such a conclusion.

Its specific character, that which marks it off from simple memory, is its tendency to selection, abstraction, and recombination. Memory, as passive, simply recalls previous experiences of objects and emotion; from these, imagination, as an active faculty, selects the elements which vividly symbolize the objects or emotions, and either by a process of abstraction allows these to do duty for the wholes, or else by a process of recombination creates new objects and new relations in which the objects stand to us or to each other (*invention*), and the result is an image of great vividness, which has perhaps no corresponding reality in the external world.

Minds differ in the vividness with which they recall the elements of previous experience, and mentally see the absent objects; they differ also in the aptitudes for selection, abstraction, recombination: the fine selective instinct of the artist, which makes him fasten upon the details which will most powerfully affect us, without any disturbance of the harmony of the general impression, does not depend solely upon the vividness of his memory and the clearness with which the objects are seen, but depends also upon very complex and peculiar conditions of sympathy which we call genius. Hence we find one man remembering a multitude of details, with a memory so vivid that it almost amounts at times to hallucination, yet without any artistic power; and we may find men—Blake was one—with an imagination of unusual activity, who are nevertheless incapable, from deficient sympathy, of seizing upon those symbols which will most affect us. Our native susceptibilities and acquired tastes determine which of the many qualities in an object shall most impress us, and be most clearly recalled. * * *

I am prepared to hear of many readers, especially young readers, protesting against the doctrine of this chapter as prosaic. They have been so long accustomed to consider imagination as peculiarly distinguished by its disdain of reality, and Invention as only admirable when its products are not simply new by selection and arrangement, but new in material, that they will reject the idea of involuntary remembrance of something originally experienced as the basis of all Art. * * *

Genius is rarely able to give any account of its own processes. But those who have had ample opportunities of intimately knowing the growth of works in the minds of artists, will bear me out in saying that a vivid memory supplies the elements from a thousand different sources, most of which are quite beyond the power of localization—the experience of yesterday being strangely intermingled with the dim suggestions of early years, the tones heard in childhood sounding through the diapason of sorrowing maturity; and all these kaleidoscopic fragments are recomposed into images that seem to have a corresponding reality of their own.

"Principles of Success in Literature," *Fortnightly Review*, I (1865), 572–579, 585–588.

II.

CULTURE AND CRITICISM

On the Science of Criticism

From Science to Criticism is a long step, yet in many quarters the question is being raised,[1] Why have we no science of Criticism? Nothing can be more patent than the fact that such a Science is absent, but I am very far from thinking that such a science is desirable. * * *

My first objection to anything like a doctrine in Literature is, that it must necessarily be so incomplete as to be tyrannically oppressive; because at the best it could only exhibit the laws which great artists had followed, it could not embrace the laws which great artists to come would follow. Thus, supposing the science perfect in its construction (a large supposition!), it could only explain the works and processes of an art that had developed itself up to a certain point; it could not explain, it could not even divine what would be the new evolutions of the art under the new conditions of advancing civilization. Let us take the case of Music, and suppose that an Aristotle had constructed a perfect science of musical criticism, out of the musical productions then known in Greece. Had there been a musical doctrine, with canons which all critics would enforce, the consequence would have been that progress would have become impossible. It is now known, and has been demonstrated, that the Greek music, from the very nature of its gamut, could have no Harmony. All the magnificent developments of modern music which spring from its enlarged gamut would, therefore, not only have been unsuspected by the critics, but would have been arrested in the early stages because "contrary to rule." The innovator would have been repressed. In like manner the Greek drama is constructed on principles so narrow compared with those of the modern drama, that an application of the canons of the one to

[1] For example, Paul Janet in "L'Esprit de discipline en Littérature . . . ," *Revue des Deux Mondes*, LXV (1866), 682–716.

the productions of the other can only be an oppressive mistake.

I have been arguing on the supposition that the Science would be a true exposition of the laws of art. If even on that supposition the effect of canons would be disastrous, what would be the effect of canons that were false? We have had one striking lesson. Europe once had a literary doctrine, which it accepted from France; and the effect of that doctrine in repressing all originality and all progress is familiarly known to the most superficial student of literary history. A somewhat similar oppression is exercised in Germany by the so-called philosophic criticism, which views a work of art in relation to certain philosophic ideas, not in relation to the effect on the emotions of the audience.

Because the Laws of Nature are more or less discoverable and reducible to a system, it is supposed that the Laws of Art must be equally discoverable. There is, however, this difference: Art is in a state of perpetual evolution, new forms arise under new conditions, and new inventions introduce new laws. Now it is certain that if men of science had the power, they would *suppress* all the facts they were unable to explain; whatever disturbed the symmetry of their doctrine would be set aside as chaotic and unworthy of a place in orderly creation. They have not this power, and so are forced reluctantly to accommodate their doctrine to the facts, to enlarge their doctrine with enlarging knowledge. But critics would have the power of suppressing originality; and would brand as "chaotic," "unworthy a place in orderly Art," whatever disturbed the symmetry of their system, whatever was not amenable to their canons.

Hence I maintain that the present state of anarchy in Criticism is preferable to a state of dogmatic authority. Criticism may suffer; but Art is freer. This is by no means asserting that one critic's judgment is as good as another's, or that every man may set up his individual judgment as a standard. One judgment is not so good as another, because it will not be founded on equal insight, equal knowledge; nor can every man make his judgment a standard for others, but only for himself and for those who think and feel like him. In every work there are certain general principles involved, and certain technical principles; the best critic is he who best understands both principles, and whose sagacity enables him to appreciate their application. The technical principles which are involved in the drama are not the same as those involved in the novel, and therefore an effect in the one may be a defect in the other. But there are certain general principles common to both, and these the public at large can judge as well as the best critic.

Inasmuch as every Art has its rules, general and technical, there might be a codification of the various rules which would be of service, and might stand for a Science of Criticism; but were this codification effected, we should still have to remember that Criticism is itself an art and not a science, and that nothing could be more disastrous than the establishment of a Doctrine of Criticism, with its rigorous canons, which would suppress originality merely because originality was a violation of some canon.

"Causeries," *Fortnightly Review*, VI (1866), 759–761.

The Criticism of Augustus Wilhelm Schlegel

The greatest of modern critics, Lessing and Winckelman, were men of great analytic power, and it is to them that we owe the best appreciation of works of art. They were not declaimers. They studied patiently, and reasoned profoundly. One aspect, one limb, did not to them represent the whole. They strove to evolve the meaning *from* each work, and not to force some *a priori* meaning *on* the work. They were judges and not advocates. It will be the scope of our remarks to show that Schlegel's "synthesis" is rash, and not founded on a due "analysis": that he is an advocate and not a judge.

The first principle of classification is to trace constant uniformities amidst varieties: applied therefore to works of art, it consists in ranging under one head all such various specimens produced by various nations as have some principle in common; so that the diversities of language, customs, and tastes, are set aside, and the real generic resemblance made the ground of classification. This would be the scientific method; but Schlegel in his celebrated classification of art into classic and romantic has acted in direct opposition to it. He has grounded his classification on a single diversity instead of a constant uniformity. Except for historical purposes, the division of art into ancient and modern is fatal: it is assuming that the spirit of art is entirely religious, whereas we hope to prove that it is *national*. The ground of classification must be ethnic not chronological: it is a question of races not of periods.

Struck with the revolution operated by Christianity in men's opinions, Schlegel and others have jumped to the conclusion, that it also operated a revolution in the *spirit* of art. This is tantamount to saying that a change of belief brings with it a change of nature and of organic tendencies. Great as must always be the influence of religion upon art, it can never entirely change

26

its spirit. Let us be understood. By the spirit of art we do not mean *opinions*. As a distinction is made, and justly, between the mind and its beliefs, so we would distinguish between the spirit of art, and the ideas therein expressed. There is in every nation an organic character, which no changes of opinion can efface; this sets its impress upon all its works, so that we never confound them with the works of another. This impress is the sign of what we call the spirit or the national tendencies of art. It cannot therefore be true that the spirit of Art is dependent on religion; the more so as religion itself is modified by the national character. We do not here allude to sectarian distinctions, or to varieties of interpretation; we point to the fact, that Christianity becomes a *subjective* religion with a northern race, while with a southern race it becomes *objective* * * *.

But while we deny that any form of religious belief can be taken as the ground of classification of works of art, we are impressed with the conviction of its influence on the national tone of thought, and consequently on the forms into which art moulds itself. What we contend for is, that the division into pagan and¸ Christian, classic and romantic, is unwarrantable; that the real distinction is national and not religious. The national distinctions are very broad. We believe they may be ranged under two general classes of objective and subjective, or of southern and northern; each class is of course to be subdivided, but the above two we regard as the most general. Let us for a moment examine the characteristics of two nations, the Italians and Germans, which may be taken as types of the two classes.

In the Italian character, feeling predominates over thought; in the German, thought predominates over feeling. * * * We use the word in no ill sense, when we call the Italian nature *sensuous*; neither do we imply any superiority when we call the German *reflective*. As far as single words can express such complex things, we believe these two express the distinctive characteristics of the nations; or we might call the former plastic and definite; the latter dreamy and vague. Every thing in Italian art is definite; in its plastic hands all things assume distinct form; Italian poetry has no *reverie*. Nothing like reverie is to be seen in the southern character; neither poetry nor music, though both so fitted to express this peculiar mental state, have been used by the southerns to express it. German art delights in it. But then the sensuous passionate nature of the Italian is averse to that dallying with thought which constitutes a reverie, while in the German it is the source of exquisite delight. The thoughts of the Italian grow quickly into passions; in the German, passions when not highly excited, have an irresistible tendency to weave themselves into thoughts: so that while in the one all ideas stimulate to action, his tendency being to throw every thing *out* of him; in the other, actions stimulate thoughts, his tendency being to connect all outward things with his inward life. * * *

In his first lecture Schlegel has given a description of what a true critic should aspire to; and this passage is worthy of being transcribed in letters of gold. "No man can be a true critic who does not possess a universality of mind, who does not possess a flexibility which, throwing aside all personal predilections and blind habits, enables him to transport himself into the peculiarities of other ages and nations, and to feel them as it were from their central point."[1] Every one has admitted the truth of this, but few have guided themselves by its light. It seems impertinent to thrust forward the truism that the foreign poet wrote to *his* nation and for *his* time, and not at all for ours—that we might as well strip him of his language as of his national peculiarities; yet this truism is perpetually being neglected; the work of the foreign poet is always judged according to our tastes and our standards. There is scarcely a critic unaware of the fact that a tragedy of the Greeks was a totally different thing from the drama of moderns; different in purpose, spirit, and execution. Nevertheless there is scarcely a critic who, judging of a Greek play, does not test it by the Shakespearean standard: talking of plot, situation, character, and passion as if the work were addressed to a modern pit of after-dinner auditors. So also the critics speak of Racine, as if he were ridiculous for not being an Englishman. Yet the man who

[1] A. W. Schlegel, *A Course of Lectures on Dramatic Art and Literature*, trans. John Black (London, 1815), I, 3.

refuses to discard his national prejudices and standards, who
refuses to regard the French poet with, as far as possible, the eyes
of a Frenchman, had better for the sake of honesty and criticism
relinquish the task altogether; otherwise he will only be illustrating Coleridge's amusing simile of the critic filling his three-ounce
phial at Niagara, and determining positively the greatness of the
cataract to be neither more nor less than his three-ounce phial
has been able to receive.[2]

We have full right to test Schlegel by his own standard; according to that we say he has shown himself to be no "true
critic," for he has failed in placing himself at the "central point
of view." We will not stop to point out the errors of his very
slovenly and inaccurate lectures on the Roman and Italian
dramas; but his treatment of Alfieri cannot be passed over in
silence.

Alfieri, the greatest of the Italian dramatists, is dismissed in
five pages, which contain almost as many blunders as paragraphs.
He is here an advocate against the poet, and very sophistical are
the arguments he brings forward. "From the tragedy of the
Greeks," he says, "with which Alfieri first became acquainted
towards the end of his career, he was separated by a wide chasm."[3]
If this be meant as expressing that the form and purpose of the
dramas of Alfieri differed from those of the ancients, it is a truism; if that the artistic spirit * * * is different, it is an absurdity. No nation so closely resembles the Greeks, in artistic spirit,
as the Italians; no dramatist so closely resembles Aeschylus as
Alfieri. "I cannot consider his pieces," continues our critic, "as
improvements on the French tragedy."[4] Why should he? Let us
for an instant grant that Alfieri is the reverse of the Greeks,
and no improvement on the French, what then? Does not the
matter resolve itself into this; that being an Italian, and addressing Italians, Alfieri is to be judged without reference to Greece
or France? His nationality is a quality, not a fault. Yet we are

[2] *Coleridge's Literary Criticism* (London: Oxford University Press, 1908)
pp. 181–182.
[3] Schlegel, *Lectures on Dramatic Art*, I, 303.
[4] *Ibid.*

told "his pieces bear no comparison with the better French tragedies in pleasing and brilliant eloquence":[5] How should they when it was his express desire to avoid declamatory tirades, which he considered undramatic? Goethe has well said that there is a negative criticism which consists in applying a different standard from that chosen by the author, and in this way you are sure to find him wanting.[6] This Schlegel perpetually uses. Alfieri hated the French, and never thought of imitating them.

It is in his account of the French Drama that Schlegel most unblushingly assumes the advocate's robe. His object is evidently not to place himself at the "central point," but to make the French drama ridiculous. He endeavours to dwarf it by most irrelevant contrasts with the Greek and Shakespearean drama, and only succeeds in displaying his critical incompetence. Let it be remembered however in extenuation, that Schlegel's object was not without its use in his day, though worse than useless now. French taste had for years usurped the German stage. Gottlob Lessing struck the usurper down.[7] By dint of rare acuteness, untiring wit, and his impetuous zeal, he won the battle for ever. Schlegel rode gracefully over the battle-field and counted the slain: then, retiring to the metropolis, published his bulletin. Beside the masculine intellect of a Lessing, clear as crystal and as solid too, Schlegel is a foppish *petit maître.* * * *

It is most true that Racine was not a Greek; true that he did not write upon romantic principles; but what then? Was he not a Frenchman, a poet of the higher order, worthy even to be placed beside the illustrious few? Because a Deer is neither Horse nor Elephant, is it nothing? It is a strange synthesis that concludes so; yet, metaphor apart, such is the conclusion of our critic. He admits that we "shall be compelled to allow the execution of the French drama is *masterly, perhaps not to be surpassed;* but the great question is, how far it is in spirit and inward essence

---

[5] *Ibid.,* p. 304.

[6] *Goethe's Literary Essays,* ed. J. E. Spingarn (New York: Harcourt, Brace, 1921), p. 140.

[7] Lessing's *Hamburgische Dramaturgie,* ed. J. Peterson (Cambridge: Cambridge University Press, 1939).

related to the Greek, and whether it deserves to be considered an improvement on it."[8] Not so at all: it is a question every way superfluous, a standard utterly fallacious. The antique drama grew up out of the spirit and artistic feeling of the Greeks, under a set of conditions which can never be again. So also did the French drama grow up out of the national spirit, of which it was the expression. It borrowed a learned air because it addressed a pedantic age; and even in its imitation of the ancients it expressed one characteristic of its own time. So also it was tinctured with gallantry, as our own drama was with concetti, because this was the fashion of the day. * * *

We can hardly hope to see many of our countrymen very hearty in their admiration of the exquisite Racine, so many obstacles are interposed; but that the feeble ridicule and ungenerous arguments of Schlegel should form another barrier to that end, is truly irritating. People talk of admiring or not admiring Racine, as if it were a matter of taste; but it is in truth a matter of knowledge. He has survived two centuries of criticism, and in spite of every change of taste; the admiration of Europe for two centuries is a pedestal whereon none but the highest can repose; those, therefore, who refuse their tribute to Racine are convicted of incompetence to judge him; convicted of want of sufficient knowledge of the language, or want of critical appreciation. Let every opponent reflect on the serious opinions once entertained by eminent Frenchmen with regard to Shakespeare. "Oh! that was ignorance!"—Granted; but does it not teach us suspicion of ourselves in judging of the French? When we hear a Frenchman disparage Shakespeare, we invariably suspect his critical power, or his knowledge of our language. * * * We have met with at least five hundred Englishmen declaring themselves "to have been mistaken for Frenchmen," so pure and fluent was their discourse; but we doubt whether more than five of them could perceive the difference between a verse of Racine and one of Quinault,[9] or between a page of George Sand and one of De

[8] Schlegel, *Lectures on Dramatic Art*, I, 319–320.
[9] Philippe Quinault (1635–1688), French dramatist, wrote libretti for Lully's operas.

Balzac; who could feel the impropriety of the celebrated *vieillard stupide* in "Hernani,"[10] or understand why the common Italian epithet *acerbo* would be inadmissible in French poetry. Here then is an obstacle to be overcome by long study alone. Beyond this there is a critical bigotry prevalent, which regards faith in Shakespeare as the only true [faith], and denounces all others as heresies. Yet surely there is room in the palace of art for more than one niche; surely we may worship Shakespeare as the sun, and yet believe Alfieri and Racine to be no inconsiderable planets?

"Augustus Wilhelm Schlegel," *Foreign Quarterly Review,* XXXII (1843), 164–179.

[10] Victor Hugo's *Hernani,* last scene of Act III.

On Style and the Imitation of Models

How is it that while every one acknowledges the importance of Style, and numerous critics from Quintilian and Longinus down to Quarterly Reviewers have written upon it, very little has been done towards a satisfactory establishment of principles? Is it not partly because the critics have seldom held the true purpose of Style steadily before their eyes, and still seldomer justified their canons by deducing them from psychological conditions? To my apprehension they seem to have mistaken the real sources of influence, and have fastened attention upon some accidental or collateral details, instead of tracing the direct connection between effects and causes. Misled by the splendour of some great renown they have concluded that to write like Cicero or to paint like Titian must be the pathway to success; which is true in one sense, and profoundly false as they understand it. One pestilent contagious error issued from this misconception, namely, that all maxims confirmed by the practice of the great artists must be maxims for the art; although a close examination might reveal that the practice of these artists may have been the result of their peculiar individualities or of the state of culture at their epoch. A true Philosophy of Criticism would exhibit in how far such maxims were universal, as founded on laws of human nature, and in how far adaptations to particular individualities. A great talent will discover new methods. A great success ought to put us on the track of new principles. But the fundamental laws of Style, resting on the truths of human nature, may be illustrated, they cannot be guaranteed by any individual success. Moreover, the strong individuality of the artist will create special modifications of the laws to suit himself, making that excellent or endurable which in other hands would be intolerable. If the purpose of Literature be the sincere expression of the individual's own ideas and feelings it is obvious that the cant about the "best models" tends to pervert and obstruct that expression. Unless a man thinks and feels precisely after the manner of Cicero and Titian it is manifestly wrong for him to express himself in their way. He may study in them the principles of effect, and try to surprise some of their secrets, but he should resolutely shun all imitation of them. They ought to be illustrations not authorities, studies not models.

The fallacy about models is seen at once if we ask this simple question: Will the practice of a great writer justify a solecism in grammar or a confusion in logic? No. Then why should it justify any other detail not to be reconciled with universal truth? If we are forced to invoke the arbitration of reason in the one case, we must do so in the other. Unless we set aside the individual practice whenever it is irreconcilable with general principles, we shall be unable to discriminate in a successful work those merits which *secured* from those demerits which *accompanied* success. Now this is precisely the condition in which Criticism has always been. It has been formal instead of being psychological: it has drawn its maxims from the works of successful artists, instead of ascertaining the pyschological principles involved in the effects of those works. When the perplexed dramatist called down curses on the man who invented fifth acts, he never thought of escaping from his tribulation by writing a play in four acts; the formal canon which made five acts indispensable to a tragedy was drawn from the practice of great dramatists, but there was no demonstration of any psychological demand on the part of the audience for precisely five acts.[1]

Although no instructed mind will for a moment doubt the immense advantage of the stimulus and culture derived from a reverent familiarity with the works of our great predecessors and contemporaries, there is a pernicious error which has been fostered by many instructed minds, rising out of their reverence for

---

[1] Lewes' note: "English critics are much less pedantic in adherence to 'rules' than the French, yet when, many years ago, there appeared a tragedy in three acts, and without a death, these innovations were considered inadmissible. . . ." Probably Lewes is here referring to his own play, *The Noble Heart* (April 16, 1849).

greatness and their forgetfulness of the ends of Literature. This error is the notion of "models," and of fixed canons drawn from the practice of great artists. It substitutes Imitation for Invention; reproduction of old types instead of the creation of new. There is more bad than good work produced in consequence of the assiduous following of models. And we shall seldom be very wide of the mark if in our estimation of youthful productions we place more reliance on their departures from what has been already done, than on their resemblances to the best artists. An energetic crudity, even a riotous absurdity, has more promise in it than a clever and elegant mediocrity, because it shows that the young man is speaking out of his own heart, and struggling to express himself in his own way rather than in the way he finds in other men's books. * * *

The French critics, who are singularly servile to all established reputations, and whose unreasoning idolatry of their own classics is one of the reasons why their Literature is not richer, are fond of declaring with magisterial emphasis that the rules of good taste and the canons of style were fixed once and for ever by their great writers in the seventeenth century. The true ambition of every modern is said to be by careful study of these models to approach (though with no hope of equalling) their chastity and elegance. That a writer of the nineteenth century should express himself in the manner which was admirable in the seventeenth is an absurdity which needs only to be stated. It is not worth refuting. But it never presents itself thus to the French. In their minds it is a lingering remnant of that older superstition which believed the Ancients to have discovered all wisdom, so that if we could only surprise the secret of Aristotle's thoughts and clearly comprehend the drift of Plato's theories (which unhappily was not clear) we should compass all knowledge. How long this superstition lasted cannot accurately be settled; perhaps it is not quite extinct even yet; but we know how little the most earnest students succeeded in surprising the secrets of the universe by reading Greek treatises, and how much by studying the universe itself. Advancing Science daily discredits the superstition; yet the advance of Criticism has not yet wholly discredited the parallel superstition in Art. The earliest thinkers are no longer considered the wisest, but the earliest artists are still proclaimed the finest. Even those who do not believe in this superiority are, for the most part, overawed by tradition and dare not openly question the supremacy of works which in their private convictions hold a very subordinate rank. And this reserve is encouraged by the intemperate scorn of those who question the supremacy without having the knowledge or the sympathy which could fairly appreciate the earlier artists. Attacks on the classics by men ignorant of the classical languages tend to perpetuate the superstition.

It will not be supposed that I would have the great writers disregarded, as if nothing were to be learned from them; but the study of great writers should be the study of general principles as illustrated or revealed in these writers; and if properly pursued it will of itself lead to a condemnation of the notion of models. What we may learn from them is a nice discrimination of the symbols which intelligibly express the shades of meaning and kindle emotions. * * * Great writers should be our companions if we would learn to write greatly; but no familiarity with their manner will supply the place of native endowment.

"Principles of Success in Literature," *Fortnightly Review*, II (1865), 259–264.

Renan and the Moral Decadence of the Age

* * * M. Renan[1] admits that at no previous period in the history of the world has there been such a clear-sighted theory of the universe and of humanity; that there is, in some thousands of our contemporaries, more penetration, insight, real philosophy, and moral delicacy than in all the previous centuries together; but this rich culture is almost without influence. A gross materialism, which only estimates things according to their immediate utility, tends more and more to assume the direction of the world, and to cast into the shade all that only serves to content the taste for the beautiful, or pure curiosity. * * * Adopt what religion or philosophy you will, he continues, man is here below for an ideal, transcendental end, something superior to mere enjoyment and material interests. But does material progress contribute to bring us nearer to such an end? Has the world, since this transformation, become on the whole more intelligent, more honest, more anxious about liberty, more sensitive to what is noble and beautiful? That is the whole question.

Truly, that is the question; and while every one will agree with him that material progress can never be considered a compensation for moral decadence, the whole force of his philippic against our age rests on the assumption that there is this moral decadence. We may be permitted to doubt the truth of this assumption. Like Mr. Carlyle, and some other writers, M. Renan takes for granted that our superiority in industrial skill has been purchased by an inferiority in other directions. But we cannot think that a dispassionate survey of the condition of England—the first of industrial nations—detects an inferiority in intelligence, morality, love of liberty, or appreciation of noble life, as compared with previous centuries. There may be a tendency in

[1] Ernest Renan in *Essais de Morale et de Critique* (Paris, 1859), pp. 22–23, 28, 356–357, 367.

some quarters to over-estimate the value of material progress. We think there is this tendency, and that it is vicious; but we have no fears that the nobler fibres of our life will cease to move us, or cease energetically to protest against such over-valuation. Look at industrial England, and ask whether the great ideas of Religion, Morality, Liberty, and Science, are banished from the minds of active men. M. Renan thinks that industry is good and honourable, but not noble. * * * Perhaps so; but does useful labour *exclude* noble life? That is the question. He considers that virtue, "genius, science, when disinterested and pursued with purely speculative aims, piety, and miliatry greatness (!) ennoble life." But who will seriously aver that these are incompatible with industrial progress? It was a favourite topic with certain writers, that England had become enervated by a long peace, until the sudden illumination of Alma, Inkermann, and Balaclava[2] revealed the folly of such declamation. And it has long been a stereotyped paragraph in French literature, that the English care only for "le *confortable*," interest themselves "aux petites choses bien plutôt qu'aux grandes idées et aux grandes passions." But is it the fact? Are we insensible to great ideas and great passions? Do we prefer comfort to freedom; do we neglect Religion, Morality, and Philosophy, for our mess of pottage? If we are not an artistic race are we therefore materialist? If the English do not interest themselves in certain "great ideas," which to the French and German mind seem of pre-eminence, it is because the English, by temperament, no less than by education, see reason to question the value and the truth of these ideas; not because industrial activity has made them forget the nobler aims of life. The Englishman is as deeply interested in religious and philosophical questions as the Frenchman or the German; but he has little faith in the representative abstractions and the metaphysical methods which occupy his neighbours. We are reproached with being a nation of shopkeepers; the truth simply being that *as* shopkeepers, we surpass other nations; and this superiority in

[2] Three famous battles fought in 1854 between the Russian and the Allied forces during the Crimean War. Tennyson's ballad on the Light Brigade commemorates the Battle of Balaclava.

industry is only *one* of the many evidences of our national power. Are we inferior as sailors, soldiers, thinkers, and writers? Is there a richer, nobler literature than our own? Are our men of science unworthy of a place beside their Continental rivals? Are our poets—in spite of our alleged unpoetical character—inferior to those of France and Germany? We have never been great in music, painting, or sculpture; but he is a bold man who will assert that, in other directions, this shopkeeping, comfort-loving, cleanly, prosaic England is inferior to any nation. * * *

Thus, then, it appears that the nation which of all others has earned the character of being an industrial nation, does *not* manifest that subjection of the higher to the lower, of the noble to the useful, of the free to the servile, which the arraigners of industrial progress declare to be inevitable. If it were devoutly believed that industry was "our being's end and aim," and if this belief could regulate life, the result would be what M. Renan asserts it actually is. But unhappily for this argument, no one does hold such a belief; and, if it were believed, the ineradicable instincts of our nature would rise as insurgents against it, and prevent the belief becoming a practical guide. So long as men have intellects, they will delight in great ideas; so long as they have sensibilities and sympathies, they will be moved by what is beautiful and good. The progress of industry cannot eradicate these. But while material progress cannot stifle moral life, it may, and many believe *must*, assist its development, by releasing man from much of his subjection to external necessities. If the labour which is done by sweat of the brow through sixteen hours of every day, can be done by a machine in three hours, the labourer has strength and leisure set free—some of which may be given to the culture of his soul. That this is no chimerical hope, is proved by the fact that, in the present day, there are thousands of artisans, who, even out of their toilsome lives find leisure and desire for intense intellectual and moral activity. No one will differ from M. Renan when he says that a fine thought, a noble sentiment, or an act of virtue, better constitutes man the king of creation, than the power of, in one instant, making known at the end of the earth his wishes or commands. But we cannot follow him when he says that while poetry exists only in the sentiments, the tendency of our epoch is to destroy poetry, by placing everywhere material instead of moral agency. The most insignificant object, the vulgarest tissue, became almost a human thing, when hundreds of human beings had breathed, felt, perhaps suffered between each throw of the shuttle, mingling their thoughts, their talk, and their songs with the work. Now an iron machine, without a soul, without beauty, has replaced all that. * * * This is what may be called the sentimental view of the question. Without denying the charm of poetical association with the spinning-wheel has for us, because it is a thing of the past, there is no evidence that poetry vanishes with the spinning-wheel. Do the weavers nowadays refrain from mingling their thoughts and sorrows, their hopes and joys, with their daily toil? And does not the poorest housewife find herself released from the toil of the wheel, because a machine is doing the work for her, and doing it better?

We must not let the ardour of argument carry us too far in our desire to vindicate the character of our national tendency. It is but too true that the inauguration of the industrial era brings with it much that is deplorable. We lose much in passing from our old and consecrated conditions. But is there not compensation for the loss? No one remembers the old days of coach-traveling without a sigh; but does he not, on the whole, prefer the railway? Much has gone, but more is gained. The spectacle of our manufacturing towns, and indeed of almost all classes of society just now, has often a depressing effect, which it requires much hopefulness or philosophy to rectify. Life has certainly become more of a struggle. And although struggles call out the energies and abilities of men, they also call out the selfishness and vanities of men. As in all struggles, the weak go to the wall, and the strong are, for the most part, too heated to be compassionate. Capital is at present a hard taskmaster. The restless desire to get rich rapidly, thwarts the very objects of wealth, which are leisure and enjoyment. To be richer than our neighbours, rather than to be better, or wiser, or happier, can never be a healthy ambition. Unhappily it is too much the ambition of our day. * * *

M. Renan loves the past and lingers fondly over every vestige which remains of the life that once was vigorous on earth. Our readers will probably share this feeling, this natural piety which links the present generations with the past. * * * It seems to us, however, that M. Renan like many others, in vindicating the claims of the past, forgets that the past itself was once a present; and if piety towards the generations that have been checks the too ready scorn or indifference which is sometimes felt and expressed for the days of old, the same piety towards the generations that are, and are to be, should check the tendency to flout and scorn our own age. Not that M. Renan is a narrow-minded worshipper of the past. "Do not let us too generously accord to the past," he says, "a moral force which has always been the appanage of but a few. Virtue diminishes or augments according as the imperceptible aristocracy in which human nobleness resides, finds or does not find an atmosphere in which to breathe and propagate." And this atmosphere, he thinks, is vitiated by industrial development. A fatal law of modern society condemns more and more the life of him who cannot produce what has a money value· The ideal of such a state is one in which every man should be a producer. "But who does not see that such a state, if it were ever constituted (which I do not believe possible), would render our planet uninhabitable for those whose duty precisely is that they should *not* sacrifice their internal liberty for a material advantage." * * *

Let us grant that the industrial element, if once it were supreme and universal, would banish from society all poetry, all liberty. Inasmuch as he admits that such an extreme case can never occur, he must believe that human beings have other feelings besides those appealed to by industrial success; and these feelings will not only demand their satisfaction, but warn us against a too precipate industrial movement. * * * It is quite clear that no good art can be produced "to order." Unless it be born and matured in the artist's own mind, it will be manufacture, not art—a *rifacimento* of existing materials, not a vision of what is new. * * * The love and vision out of which a work will issue, cannot be commanded—cannot even be willed by the artist himself. Thus, whether the artist find a purchaser for what has issued out of this love and vision, or whether no one but himself will ever prize it, the money, or no money, which may reward his labours, is a subsequent, and as respects art, indifferent matter. The creation of art is not industrialism. The disposal of a work of art is. All the gold of California would be insufficient to buy a single poem, or a single picture, unless the poet and the painter had seen and suffered what their art expressed. All that industrialism can do to favour art, is by stimulating the artist to labour more; and all that it can do to deteriorate art, is by seducing the artist to become a rapid manufacturer.

Grant that art cannot be produced "to order," that the artist must first *be* an artist, and create because the faculties within him imperiously demand exercise, and the question of whether he shall be paid in money, becomes quite subsidiary. A brave strong man, beholding another struggling with flames or the waves, rushes to the rescue, because he is prompted by sympathy, not because the grateful man will perhaps reward that assistance in money. No sum of money will tempt the coward, or the unfeeling man. And if the consciousness that a large reward will follow, does mingle with the motives which urge a man to the rescue of his fellow—if it act as a stimulus, this is surely not a matter for regret. Yet M. Renan is apparently of those who would regret it. He seems to believe that the fact of an artist being paid tends to degrade art. * * * Yet history has another story to tell. Stephenson was not poor; Watt was not poor. Shakespeare, Goethe, Michael Angelo, Raphael, and Rubens managed to secure their share of the good things of this life, without missing the reward of glory. In fact, as we before hinted, the artist produces his work because he is an artist; whether or not that work will be rewarded in hard cash and present renown, depends upon a variety of conditions; but paid and applauded, or unpaid and neglected, he will work on, if the noble impulse lives within him.

On the whole, therefore, we cannot agree in the somewhat

gloomy view which M. Renan takes of our age and its industrial tendencies. We can understand how his meditative pensive spirit may be depressed by the spectacle of much that it contemplates, especially in France. We can sympathize with his protest against the political and moral lassitude, which would abdicate the nobler strivings in favour of a servile contentedness with some material advantages. We can even understand that such a voice of warning may not be without its effect. But our more hopeful minds refuse to accept his sombre descriptions. Sharing his repugnance at the idea of an industrial supremacy which would paralyze moral and intellectual vigour, we do not believe such a supremacy to be probable, we do not believe Europe likely to forego its birthright for the mess of pottage.

"Another Pleasant French Book," *Blackwood's*, LXXXVI (1859), 672–677.

A Frenchman, an Englishman, and a German

A Frenchman, an Englishman, and a German were commissioned, it is said, to give the world the benefit of their views on that interesting animal the Camel. Away went the Frenchman to the *Jardin des Plantes,* spent an hour there in rapid investigation, returned and wrote a *feuilleton,* in which there was no phrase the Academy could blame, but also no phrase which added to the general knowledge. He was perfectly satisfied, however, and said, *Le voila, le chameau!* The Englishman packed up his tea-caddy and a magazine of comforts; pitched his tent in the East; remained there two years studying the Camel in its habits; and returned with a thick volume of facts, arranged without order, expounded without philosophy, but serving as valuable materials for all who came after him. The German, despising the frivolity of the Frenchman, and the unphilosophic matter-of-factness of the Englishman, retired to his study, there *to construct the Idea of a Camel from out of the depths of his Moral Consciousness.* And he is still at it.

The Life of Goethe (3rd ed.; London: Smith, Elder, 1875), p. 397.

III.

POETRY AND POETS: ANCIENT AND MODERN

What Is Poetry?

* * * *What is poetry?* Have there not been innumerable essays, disquisitions, discussions, definitions and prefaces on this subject, and are we nearer the mark? Alas, no! The only cheering sign in the whole matter is the restlessness, which, not satisfied with these vague generalities, ever prompts men to fresh attempts. This is an old question, and one which, from its very simplicity and our familiarity with its subject, is not easily analysed. Hence the vagueness and inapplicability of all definitions. Men do not look steadily and patiently *at* the thing, but follow its shifting lights, dancing now here, now there, and give us but a sense of their own uneasiness for result. Thus when Schlegel calls it "the mirror of ideas eternally true," he is not only wrong (as we shall see), but extremely vague—what application can be made of such a definition? Schiller does not advance the matter by calling it "the representation of the supersensuous." Aristotle's celebrated dictum of poetry being an "imitative art," does not distinguish it from the other arts, and is moreover false. To say poetry is an imitative art is saying nothing if true, but it is not true. An image is defined by Quatremère de Quincy to be "morally speaking the same as its model, though physically it is some other," and imitation is "to produce the resemblance of a thing, but in some other thing which becomes the image of it."[1] This is the best possible explanation for Aristotle, and yet it does not render his definition correct. Poetry is *substitutive* and suggestive, not imitative; *words,* not *images,* are employed; nor let it be supposed, as it too generally is, that words raise the images in our

[1] Friedrich von Schlegel, *Athenäum* (Berlin: Vieweg Frölich, 1798–1800), I, Part 2, pp. 28 ff. F. Schiller, "Upon the Pathetic," *Essays Aesthetical and Philosophical* (London, 1879), pp. 142 ff.; Quatremère de Quincy, *Essay on the Nature, the End, and the Means of Imitation in the Fine Arts,* trans. J. C. Kent (London, 1837) pp. 11 and 13.

minds—they seldom, if ever, raise an *image* of the *thing*, often no images at all, as some of the finest passages will evidence. Compare Æschylus, Milton, or Shakespeare on this point. "It is one thing to make an idea clear, and another to make it *affecting* to the imagination." What *images* does Milton's description of Death call up?

> The other shape,
> If shape it might be call'd that shape had none
> Distinguishable in member, joint or limb;
> Or substance might be call'd that shadow seem'd,
> For each seem'd either; black he stood as night;
> Fierce as ten furies—terrible as hell.

If poetry is an imitative art—imitative of what? of external reality? images of what? of things seen or felt? Of what is the above passage imitative? "Whoever attentively considers the best passages of poetry will find that it does not in general produce its end by raising the images of things, but by *exciting a passion similar to that which real objects will excite by other means.*"[2] This is profoundly true, and goes to the root of the matter. Even in description, when imitation would naturally be more close, the poet does *not* present images of the thing described. "Descriptive poetry consists, no doubt, in description, but in description of things as they *appear*, not as they *are*; and it paints them, not in their bare natural lineaments, but arrayed in the colours and seen through the medium of the imagination set in action by the feelings. If a poet is to describe a lion, he will not set about it as a naturalist would, intent on stating the truth, but by suggesting the most striking likenesses and contrasts *which might occur to a mind contemplating the lion* in the state of awe, wonder, or terror, which the spectacle naturally excites."[3] The error we are

[2] Lewes himself calls attention to Burke's "On the Sublime and the Beautiful," Pt. II, Sec. 3, 4, 5 and Pt. V, Sec. 5, 6, 7. The quotation from *Paradise Lost,* Bk. II, ll. 666–671, Oxford Edition, appears in the Burke essay.

[3] J. S. Mill, "What Is Poetry?" *Monthly Repository,* VII (1833), 63. See A. T. Kitchel, *George Lewes and George Eliot* (New York: John Day, 1933), pp. 30 ff. for the correspondence between Mill and Lewes on the Hegel article.

uprooting is deeply seated and far-spread; its traces are constantly visible in criticism; and it was so firmly believed in by Dr. Darwin, that he made it the groundwork of his poetry. A signal instance of his misapprehension occurs in the *Botanic Garden,* where he thus criticises Pope: "Mr. Pope has written a bad verse in the Windsor Forest,

> And Kennet swift, for silver eels *renown'd.*

The word *renown'd does not present the idea of a visible object to the mind,* and thence is prosaic. But change the line thus,

> And Kennet swift, where silver graylings *play.*

it becomes poetry, because the scenery is then brought before the eye."[4] If this were once admitted it would sweep away the finest poetry, and substitute *an animated catalogue* of things. This error is, as indeed is all error, an incomplete truth. It is true in part, and only false when applied to the *whole.* An image that is addressed to the *eye* should of course be clear and defined, or it is useless. Images in poetry are used to intensify, or render intelligible that which would otherwise not be so clear, and therefore a *visual* object may be brought to illustrate one that is not visual —but when thus selected it should be correct. So far Darwin's theory is admissible; but he makes the grand mistake of supposing that *all* images in poetry must be addressed to the eye; forgetting that the other senses, physical and moral (so to speak), are also addressed. Poetry then is not an imitative art, in any sense which may be legitimately given to imitation; nor can we think, with the Marquis de Santillana, that it is an invention of "useful things," which, being enveloped in a beautiful veil, are arranged, exposed and concealed according to a certain calculation, measurement and weight. * * *[5] Our English critics talk elaborately

[4] Erasmus Darwin, *Botanic Garden: The Loves of the Plants, Interlude I.*

[5] "E que cosa es la poesia que en nuestro vulgar *Gaya Sciencia* . . . llamamos, si non un fingimiento de cosas utiles cubiertas, ò veladas con muy fermosa cobertura, compuestas, distinguidas, è scandidas por cierto cuento, peso, è medida?" Marques de Santillana, *Proemio al Condestable de Portugal* in T. A. Sanchez, ed., *Coleccion de poesias castellanas anteriores al siglo XV* (Madrid, 1779), I, XLIX–L.

about its being derived from ποιέω, and meaning *creation*—whereupon many rhetorical flourishes, and the thing is done! * * *

We think Poetry demands two separate definitions, each the complement to the other.

1. Its *abstract* nature, *i.e.* Art as Art—the "spirit which informs" architecture, sculpture, painting, music and poetry, considered in its abstract existence.

2. Its *concrete* nature, *i.e.* poetry as an individual art, and as such distinguished from the others, and from all forms of thought whatever. These definitions we offer as

1. *Poetry is the beautiful phasis of a religious Idea.*

2. *Poetry is the metrical utterance of emotion.* [This either expressive of emotion in itself, or calculated to raise emotion in the minds of others.] These two definitions, united into one general definition, may therefore stand thus:—the metrical utterance of emotion, having beauty for its result, and pervaded by a religious Idea which it thereby symbolizes.

The wording of these definitions may be questionable, and they require elucidation: the first may be called *the religious Idea incarnate in the beautiful*; but any formula must needs be elucidated: and this we proceed to attempt—till after which we beg the reader to suspend his judgment. The second we must consider first. Poetry must be emotive, it must be metrical—these are its conditions.

The domain of Art is not the intellect, but the emotions—not thought, but feeling; it occupies itself with thoughts only as they are associated with feelings; as Bettina profoundly says, "art is the intuition of spirit into the senses. *What you feel becomes thought, and what you strive to invent becomes sensual feeling;*"[6] and thus, as Coleridge and Wordsworth have long taught, the true antithesis to poetry is not prose, but *science.* "Poetry is the breath and finer spirit of all knowledge; the impassioned expression which is in the countenance of science."[7] Thoughts do and must abound in all good poetry, but they are there not for their

---

[6] Goethe's *Briefwechsel mit einem kinde* (Berlin, 1881), p. 381.

[7] Wordsworth's Preface to the *Lyrical Ballads.*

own sake, but for the *sake of a feeling*; a thought is sometimes the *root,* of which the feeling is the *flower,* and sometimes the *flower,* of which feeling is the *root.* Thought for thought's sake is science —thought for feeling's sake, and feeling for feeling's sake are poetry. * * *

It is this emotive principle which creates all the ornaments, as they are styled, such as personification, metaphor and trope; for nothing being announced as a fact, but everything as seen through the passionate medium of the speaker's soul, it necessitates a figurative impassioned language. * * * "Ornaments" may be used by imitators and verse-makers, but they are always foreign, repulsive and cumbersome, simply because they *are* ornaments ostentatiously worn for their glitter, and not *real associations* clinging round the central feeling. But in the true poet, imagination acting on the feeling, or the feeling acting on the imagination, condenses and fuses a whole series of ideas into one *nexus* of expression; such is personification, one of the most poetical of figures, but which, when not springing from the ground of real passion, becomes an impertinence in the imitator or scholar-poet, and warms the mind no more than prose. When Milton speaks of

> The *starry Galileo* in his woes,[8]

it is as if lightning flashed on the whole dark career of the man; all the scattered rays of light which have played around his name, his discoveries and his misfortunes are converged into one focus, and stand burning inextinguishably there. This is an instance of true passionate expression. Byron, in his celebrated stanzas on the Dying Gladiator, has given as striking an instance of the false expression—the merely *recherché* illustration suggested by thought or perception of analogies purely intellectual:

> And through his side the last drops ebbing slow
> From the red gash, fall heavy, one by one,
> *Like the first of a thunder shower.*[9]

[8] Lewes is mistaken here. "The Starry Galileo with his woes" is from Byron's *Childe Harold's Pilgrimage,* Canto IV, stanza 54.

[9] *Childe Harold's Pilgrimage,* Canto IV, stanza 140.

Nothing can be more forced than the comparison of drops of blood to drops of rain. Note also the antithesis of *last* drops of blood and *first* drops of rain. The common epithet "snowy bosom" is another example. Marino in Italy, and Gongora in Spain, as well as Cowley and Donne in England, only pushed this principle into a system, and the result was affectation or wit. It is against such ornaments, and the vicious *Gongorism* they induced, that Wordsworth's theory was virtually directed; and although he was radically wrong in saying poetry differed in nothing from prose, yet we confess that such ornaments as coquettes put on the bosoms of their verses are but as gauds to hide the wrinkled skin on which they glitter; still those who, in their fury of simplicity—who, in their disgust at dowager-diamonds, declare that a lovely maiden shall not place a rose in her hair, because ornament is unnecessary, commit a sad blunder, and slight the beautiful because the deformed will ape it. Wordsworth, in consequence, often writes passages worthlessly prosaic. Nevertheless, although *prosaic*, such are not *prose*, simply because of their metrical expression; and this leads us to the second point of our inquiry, viz., the essential position of verse.

Verse is the form of poetry; not the form as a thing *arbitrary,* but as a thing vital and essential; it is the incarnation of poetry. To call it the *dress,* and to consider it apart as a thing distinct, is folly, except in technical instruction. Rhythm is not a thing invented by man, but a thing *evolved* from him, and it is not merely the accidental form, but the only possible form of poetry; for there is a rhythm of feeling correspondent in the human soul. * * *

Poetry then, we agree with Wordsworth, is not the antithesis to prose, neither is animal the antithesis to plant; but a generic difference exists, which it is always fatal to overlook. Verse is not synonymous with poetry, but is the incarnation of it; and prose may be emotive—poetical, but never poetry. To those who assert, that all that is said in verse might be equally said in prose, we answer, as soon might cabbages be violets; we may as well object to the restricted size of the violet, forgetting its odour, or to its want of utility, forgetting its beauty. * * *

We have now disposed of the second, or *technical* part of our definition, and are now in a condition to examine the first part—*the beautiful phasis of a religious Idea.*

The word "beautiful" itself might challenge a definition, were it not sufficiently intelligible from the context; but *"pleasurable"* might also be substituted. That the medium of Art must necessarily be the Beautiful, no one doubts; but unfortunately this dictum is not sufficiently applied in criticism, or the Deformed and Disgusting would not so often have been suffered to pass. "The world of art," says Jean Paul, "must be the highest, the most ideal, wherein every pang dissolves into greater pleasure, and where we resemble men on mountain-tops; the storm which bursts heavily on the real life and world below, is to us but as a cooling shower. Hence every poem is unpoetical, as every song is unmusical that ends with a discord."[10] It is indeed another world, wherein our own is reflected, but idealized; and in its struggles and battles no blood flows from the wounded foot soldier, but celestial *ichor* from a wounded god. This is triumphantly shown in music—

Yearning like a god in pain[11]

as Keats so beautifully says, where the most plaintive melodies—strains that move the heart to tears, are still always tempered into rapture by the pervading spirit of beauty. There is a song in the mind of every true poet which likewise tempers his painful thoughts; and the great poet is nowhere more recognizable than in this song, which gives him free movement in the absurdly called *"shackles"* of verse. Wherever you discern the "shackles," you may be sure the mind is a captive, and no golden eagle "wantoning in the smile of Jove." You discern the shackles by the "fillings up," by the irrelevancies introduced for the sake of a rhyme, etc.

If this be admitted, it strikes at the root of Wordsworth's theory of poetic diction, since the condition imposed of a beauti-

[10] Johann Paul Friedrich Richter, *Vorschule der Aesthetik: Jean Pauls Werke,* ed. R. Wustmann (Leipzig: Bibliographisches Institut, 1908), IV, 124.
[11] Keats, "Eve of St. Agnes," stanza 7, l. 2.

ful medium, requires that the diction be not "the ordinary language of mankind," but a language fitted to the ideal mouths it issues from; and this must not be done alone by figurative, passionate, or personified phrases, but by an abstraction of all mean and ludicrous words. Certain associations cling round certain words, and the poet must comply with these; if they be ridiculous he must avoid them, because the reader cannot escape the unlucky associations. Suppose a version of the Iliad opening thus—

> *John Thompson's wrath* to us the direful spring.

Or the *Orlando Furioso* thus—

> The Wilsons, Smiths, the Wigginses and Browns.

Yet this is scarcely an exaggeration on a sonnet[12] of Wordsworth's, commencing—

> Spade with which Wilkinson has till'd his land!

Now we defy the reader to be pleasurably moved by *Wilkinson*; the name is a name "comme un autre," and no doubt denotes many a respectable family, but the gods have not decreed it poetical; on the contrary, its abundant use by comic writers, coupled to its oddity as a sound, have consecrated it to fun, and not to poetry—sonnets least of all. Wilkinson is, therefore, a violation of the ideal. "Achilles' wrath" does very well. Achilles is an ideal personage, of whom, had we previously known nothing, we might predicate what greatness we pleased; but "John Thompson" is the name of our butcher, or who sat next to us in the pit last night, or sent a begging-letter—how *can* the name denote ideal character? It is useless arguing the point with the public: Harry Gill and Betty Foy *do* excite the ludicrous, and destroy all impression of poetry. Wordsworth is so insensible to this, or so obstinate in his theory, that he mingles risibilities and puerilities with magnificent and intense poetry.

We have now to consider it in the light of one *phasis of a religious Idea.*

---

[12] From Wordsworth's *Poems of Sentiment and Reflection*; the poem referred to is not a sonnet.

No nation hitherto known has been without its poetry; but then does this potent universality indicate nothing? has poetry had no other end than the one actually alleged—amusement? or is it true, as is often said, that "the arts spring from the natural propensities of mankind, and *fill up the idle hour of the savage as well as that of the more luxurious civilized nation?*" This opinion, which could only have arisen in the mind of a dry logician, degrades Art to a mere doll and fancy-fair production; but fortunately the logic is as false as it is degrading. It is a confusion of means with an end. "The pleasure that the organ receives," says Quatremère de Quincy, "is indeed one of the ends of art, since, if that pleasure did not exist, the action of the art itself would be as if it were not. But that such can be its true end, is one of the errors arising from ignorance and thoughtlessness; as well might it be maintained that the pleasure derived from eating is the end of that want, while it is surely nothing more than a means of attaining another pleasure, that of health, strength and the use of our faculties. The pleasure is a means which nature herself has placed as an incentive to those appetites, that lead the way to the accomplishment of all her designs."[13]

The opinion often advocated in Germany and France, of "Art for Art's sake," of Art's knowing no end beyond itself, is a little better, but we think equally incorrect, and equally confounding means with an end; for in looking narrowly at the history of poetry, we find everywhere one determinate element and condition, which we hold to be the soul of Art, and this is its religious Idea. Every poet stands at the head of his age at once its child and prophet; and the psalm which breaks solemnly from him, however varied by the music of his feelings, ever retains the one burthen—*elevation of the race he addresses into a higher sphere of thought.* * * *

Be it observed, that so far from poetry being the "mirror of ideas eternally true," it must, on the contrary, ever be the mirror of *truths of periods,* because the poet cannot but see through the

---

[13] Quatremère de Quincy, *Essay on the Nature, the End, and the Means of Imitation in the Fine Arts,* p. 180.

medium of his age, cannot see *much* beyond it, but must inevitably, if he would get a hearing, utter its spirit and wisdom in their highest point. What is truth? How is it to be stamped with eternity? Where is its criterion? The truth of today is the doubt of tomorrow; how then can the poet *get at* this eternal truth? That which alone is eternally true to human cognizance is human passion and this is the evergreen of poetry. The wild war-song of the savage is undoubtedly poetry; and although the barbarity, cunning and ferocity it praises and inculcates are, to an advanced civilization, very revolting, they are to the savage the highest wisdom. "It was an ancient custom among the Arabs to celebrate the valour and noble deeds of great men. *Nor is there any kind of poetry more useful.* For nothing is more edifying to stir up the spirit and to excite it to virtues, nothing furthermore is more efficacious for achieving that end than to bring forth those examples *which the reader may admire and propose to himself for imitation.*"[14] Homer expressly states, that glorious actions and noble destinies are the substance of poetry; and Pierre Vidal, the celebrated Troubadour, in his advice to one of his brethren as to the mode of exercising the profession, also teaches this. * * *[15]

These citations, which might be indefinitely multiplied, are sufficient to show how impressed men have been from all times with the great *moral* influence of poetry; but this moral influence in final analysis becomes a religious Idea. By a religious Idea we do not mean the formalized religion of the epoch, nor even an acknowledged part of it, but, *more Germanico*, regard every Idea as partaking essentially of the religious character, which is the formula of any truth leading to new contemplations of the infinite, or to new forms in our social relations. Thus liberty, equal-

[14] "Poëseos Asiaticae" in *The Works of Sir William Jones* (London, 1807), IV, 294: "Celebrare res praeclare gestas ac virorum fortium virtutes antiqua fuit Arabibus consuetudo. *Neque est ullum poëseos genus utilius*: nihil enim est praestabilius quam animum ad virtutes impellere atque incendere, nihil porro ad eum finem consequendum efficacius, quam ea proferre exempla, *quae lector admiretur et sibi imitanda proponat.*"

[15] *Iliad*, vi, 358; *Odyssey*, iii, 204; xxiv, 197; J. C. L. Simonde de Sismondi, *De la littérature du Midi de l 'Europe* (2nd ed.: Paris, 1819), I, 179; Claude Millot, *Histoire littéraire des troubadors* (Paris, 1802), II, 283 ff.

ity, humanity (the threefold form of this century's mission), are not, so to speak, "doctrinal points" in the formalized religion of the epoch; but inasmuch as they express (in the final analysis) the object and faith of the crusade in which all Europe is now sensibly or insensibly engaged, and as they have to complete a great social end, so may they be considered as eminently religious. We caution the reader against any narrow or exclusive interpretation of our expressions; nor must he be hasty in making his application of them. We admit that the poet does not give to this Idea its naked expression, nor is he even conscious of it; such is the task of the philosopher. Moreover, although we use the word Idea in its highest abstract sense, as expressing *potentially* the whole spirit of the age, yet we are aware of how many antagonistic different elements it is made up, and consequently each poem will mostly contain but one or more of these elements; not the entire Idea. * * *16

If our theory be false, if there be no idea lying beneath the expression, and if poetry be the mere expression of feeling for feeling's sake, how comes it that all times do not alike produce poets? How is it that poetry arises in cycles, gets its doctrine uttered by half a dozen men, and then slumbers for centuries, to arise again with pristine vigour? *Accident* is a favourite theory, but an untenable one. Look at history, and see if the indications be not too universal and too regular for accident. It has been repeatedly remarked, that it is not in times of luxurious idleness and fat peace, but in those of conflict and trouble, that the arts have been most flourishing. Look at Athens, that perpetual struggle of men. Look at Italy in the days of Dante and Petrarca, distracted by factions, wars and contentions of all kinds. Look at England under Elizabeth and James (which was the new birth of an era,—Protestantism accepted and believed after its fierce strug-

---

16 Lewes' note: "It will have been apparent that we have used the word 'Idea' in its European philosophical sense, as the synthetical expression of each great element of the spirit of the age. Thus analysis was the dominant Idea of the eighteenth century; humanity (liberty, progression) of the nineteenth. Feudalism, monarchism, protestantism, catholicism, etc. are but formulas which we name Ideas."

gle), also after the Rebellion, and after the French revolution. Wherever you cast your eyes, the same phenomenon presents itself. The reason is, that *every revolution or internal change is the birth of a creed which is felt by the whole mass*; the philosophers have long known the ideas contained therein, but the revolution is the result of the participation of the mass of mankind; the poet arises to utter the collective creed, with its hopes for the future. He does not, as we before hinted, give this Idea its naked expression; and indeed (unless the word *poet* be used as the abstract and expression of the whole voice of poetry at any time) he does not either feel or comprehend this Idea in its completeness, but only in one or more phases thereof: hence the necessity for more than one singer; hence Wordsworth, Coleridge, Shelley, Byron, Rogers, Campbell, Keats, Moore, Crabbe, etc. were each necessary to the completing of the Idea of their epoch; and hence also the reason of the crowds of imitators, successful and otherwise, who walk in the footsteps of a newly arisen poet. Their inarticulate yearnings and thoughts they have found articulate in his works, and they join their voices in the plaintive wail, the Titanic struggle, or jubilant hope, uttering *similar* thoughts rather than imitating his. Every man that has a real insight of more or less depth, is something more than an imitator; for he helps to complete that portion of the Idea at which he works. An Idea is not the work of one man, but of many; not of one day, but of an epoch; and each one gives it his own imperfect formula. The great poet may feel it in its totality more intensely than another, but no one man can complete it. If then, as Hegel says, the key to the philosophy and religion of a nation is to be found in its poetry, so we may reverse it, and say that the philosophical Idea of an epoch being given, we have at once the key to its poetry. Indeed no criticism on a past epoch's poetry can be significant without a clear conception of the dominant Idea of that epoch, and it is owing to the neglect of this that so much nonsense has been written on the ancients. Let us not be misunderstood: we repeat again and again, that the poet does not, cannot give the scientific accuracy or expression to the Idea—this is the province of philosophy; but *the Idea must ever, in one of its grand or minute phases, be the basis of his poem*; and moreover as there are many conflicting Ideas in every epoch, the various poets will severally express them, but the dominant one alone carries immortality with it.

Holding these opinions, we cannot but look favourably on the fact of the march of intellect having been followed by the diffusion of poetry, and however we may be for the moment irritated at the self-sufficiency and presumption of the *dii minores*, whose verses manufactured for the day are forgotten on the morrow, and whose "pretensions widen every smile their imbecility excited," because such pretensions must always be ridiculous; yet apart from these, no one, we think, can be indifferent to the daily increasing influence and production of poetry. As religion in earliest times was expounded by a few priests, and was *understood* by them alone, but has now, through its Christian development, become intelligible and practical to millions; so poetry, in becoming thus diffused, is developing its mission, widening its influence, and daily becoming a more potent element of life. Most foolish is the cry, "that poetry is dead," or "poetry's a drug." Poetry never dies, never becomes a drug, and least of all now, when every day brings fresh writers, and every day republications in all possible forms and at all prices of all possible writers. * * * Poetry will one day become one of the elements of life— a sixth sense more keen and important than all the rest.

Life is earnest, art is serene.[17]

But it is a noble dream, if a dream, to elevate life itself into the spiritual clearness and ideality of Art. Deep and beautiful is the advice of Goethe, that we should "every day hear a little song, see a good picture, read some poetry, and, if possible, talk some sensible words,"[18] that we may thus cultivate a harmony of soul, which must eventually express itself in life. * * *

"Hegel's Aesthetics: Philosophy of Art," *British and Foreign Review,* XIII (1842), 5–30.

[17] "Ernst ist das Leben, heiter ist die Kunst," Schiller, Prologue, *Wallensteins Lager, Schiller Werke* (Berlin: Paul Stapf, 1962), I. 558.

[18] *Wilhelm Meister's Apprenticeship,* trans. Carlyle, Bk. V, chap. I.

Homer

The difficulty of supposing several men of genius equal to
that displayed in the Homeric poems, arises solely from what we
cannot but regard as a misconception of the nature of that
genius; a very natural misconception indeed, but one which a
little scrutiny would dispel. To conceive two Virgils, two Dantes,
two Miltons, or two Goethes, would indeed be difficult; but we
find no difficulty in conceiving twenty Homers, though we think
the *Iliad* and *Odyssey* as great as the *Aeneid,* the *Divine Comedy,
Paradise Lost,* or *Faust.* We make a distinction between the superiority of the poem, and the superiority of the poet. It may
look like an idle paradox to say so, but we are firmly convinced
that an analysis of the pleasure given by the Homeric poems,
while it in nowise diminished our admiration for those poems,
would greatly diminish our admiration for their author, or authors. Let us be understood. All early ages are poetical; their
language is vitally metaphorical—unconsciously so. In the infancy
of society, as Shelley says, every author is necessarily a poet, because language itself is poetry.[1] Every original language, near to
its source, is in itself the chaos of a cyclic poem: the copiousness
of lexicography, and the distinctions of grammar, are the works
of a later age. Beyond this the early poet lives in a free com-
munion with nature. * * * He lives in a society where all the
passions are freely and undisguisedly exhibited, and wherein
adventure is the condiment of life. Moreover, the vast field of
invention is open to him; he is not bound to follow in the footsteps of the poets who have gone before him, and so to distort
truth for the sake of appearing original.

   * * * Let us here ask,—Are not the great qualities of the
Homeric poems precisely the qualities which such conditions
would foster: vivid imagery, clear pictures, healthy vigour, *naï-*

[1]Shelley's *A Defence of Poetry.*

veté, simple passions, and untrammelled originality? These qualities, which the modern poet can only attain by the subtleties of consummate art, and then never in the same perfection, in the Homeric poet were spontaneous; he uttered such poetry because he could utter no other, and his simple utterance was poetry. Give him great, though not rare sensibility, a large musical soul, such as hundreds are gifted with, and he will pour forth that sort of poetry which forms the wonder and delight of after ages—an *Iliad*, a *Niebelungen Lied*, or a *Romancero*. If it be objected, that the *Iliad* surpasses all similar works, and is, therefore, not fairly classed with them, the answer is, that its superiority is not more striking than we have reason to expect from so gifted and so splendid a race as the Greeks, who reached perfection in so many paths. If it be objected, that the Homeric epics surpass the cyclic epics, the answer is, that the celebrity of the Homeridæ *was grounded on that superiority*. In our own day, we have seen such poets as Scott, Wordsworth, Coleridge, Southey, Byron, Moore, Shelley, Keats, Leigh Hunt, &c., as contemporaries; and no wonder is excited at their superiority over the numerous crowd of poetical aspirants.

Admitting, then, all that is claimed for the Homeric poems, in the shape of transcendent poetry, we still see no reason to regard the authors as miraculous poets; the more so, as it is generally forgotten, in this argument, how much our delight in the poems is purely critical and historical: traits of simplicity, indications of early barbarism, pictures of a bygone creed and a bygone civilization, which rouse us to raptures of delight, and yet are no merits in the poet. We always read the poem with a secret understanding that we are to find in it the expression of an antique period, and do not, therefore, demand from it the refinements of modern poetry, the qualities of modern art; nor are we shocked at *any* faults, *any* rudenesses, *any* tautologies. The very faults for which we should pitilessly condemn a Virgil or a Milton, become positive sources of delight when we meet with them in Homer. In Homer, artlessness has the effect of exquisite art. But *is* it art? This is the point assumed: because Homer gives greater delight than Virgil, he is pronounced a greater artist; which is preposterous. One might almost as well say, that because a real peach is more delicious to the taste than a painted imitation would be, the gardener is a greater artist than the painter. Homer, like all early poets, can scarcely be said to feign: he writes things, not words; and in his day all things were vivified with imagination. Later poets have to imitate things *that were,* because reason has remorselessly slain the

> Fair humanities of old religion.
> And to yon starry home they now are gone,
> Spirits or Gods, that used to share this earth
> With man as with their friend.[2]

The later poet has to create, by art, something of the effect which the early poet created, by a rude untutored utterance of the thoughts and feelings that were struggling within him.

We know not whether we make our argument intelligible; but it seems to us impossible for any dispassionate reader of Homer not to be struck with the excessive rudeness and artlessness of his style—with the absence of any great o'ermastering individuality, which, were it there, would set its stamp upon every line, as in Dante, Milton, or Shakespeare—with the absence, in short, of everything that can, properly speaking, be called art. People, indeed, talk of the exquisite delineation of character. We cannot see it. The characters are *true;* but they are merely outlined. They are to the characters of Shakespeare—to which rash admiration has sometimes compared them—as the rude outline of a figure on the wall is to the perfect sculpture of a Phidias. The passions, indeed, are finely portrayed; but what poet, in any age, has failed *there?* Homer uses the most melodious and flexible language known; yet much of his verse is a mere jingle, and is stuffed out with idle epithets and particles, or with tautologies, merely thrust in to keep up the jingle. If any one will maintain that the style—i.e., the language—of the *Iliad* is like that of artistic poets, we cannot argue with him—we cease all attempts at convincing him; but we must doubt whether so hardy a critic can be found. And if the language be given up, the whole point is given

---

[2] Schiller, *Wallenstein,* Pt. I, II, 2.

up; because language is the touchstone of poetic art, since it is the only thing which the before-mentioned conditions, surrounding and influencing the early poet, cannot bestow, and which, even in later poets, marks at once the distinction between the real artist and the bungling imitator.

"Art is form and nothing else," says George Sand, with profound insight. To the same purport Goethe—

> In the contemplation of Art
> You must ever regard the one as the all.
> Nothing is inner, nothing is outer,
> For what is within that is without.[3]

* * * This doctrine will with difficulty be accepted in England, where an unreasonable contempt for style is usually paraded, owing to the fallacy that the form of a poem is like a dress, something put on, whereas it is a shape in which thoughts and feelings incarnate themselves. The distinction between simple poetical emotion and poetical art, is the distinction between feeling and creating. Thousands who have poetical thoughts are unable to incarnate them in appropriate expressions;—they are not poets. If, therefore, the art of a poet consists in this operation—this *Gestaltung*—it follows that the true test of the artist is to be found in his style; and style is perfect, in as far as it is the most beautiful and appropriate shape which the thoughts can assume. Sonorous words may be sonorous nothings; splendid images may be like jewels upon a ragged beggar; and thus the versifier, though dealing with the gems he has stolen from the coronets of real poets, cannot conceal the theft—cannot get himself accepted as a poet; because the poet is known, not by his sonorous epithets, not by his dazzling images, not even by his original conceptions, but by his style, by the exquisite form in which his thoughts

[3] "L'art est une forme; et rien autre chose," George Sand, *Les Sept Cordes de la Lyre* (Paris, 1869), p. 28; "Müsset in dem Kunst betrachten/ Immer eins wie Alles achten,/ Nichts ist drinnen, Nichts ist draussen;/ Denn was *innen* das ist *aussen.*" Goethe's "Epirrhema," in *Goethe Werke* (Berlin: Paul Stapf, 1962), I, 436. Lewes substitutes "in dem Kunst betrachten" for Goethe's actual lines "im Naturbetrachten," which would not be relevant since Lewes is discussing art, not nature.

are fashioned. If sonorousness and imagery could make a poet, Montgomery would be one; if original conception could make a poet, Hoffmann[4] and Mrs. Shelley would have precedence over Homer, Milton, or Shakespeare; if the invention and disposition of an interesting story could be put forward as claims, Alexander Dumas is immeasurably superior to Wordsworth; if the portrayal of character be a test, Balzac and Miss Austen are greater than all the modern poets. We might go through the list of qualities, and we should still find that in each the poet was rivalled and excelled by some writer not a poet, until we come to style, and style is inimitable, indestructible—the only final test of a poet's *art*. * * * Now Homer's style is unquestionably that of a poet, not that of an imitator; it is vivid, graphic, direct, and adapted to the thoughts; but it is at the same time rude, careless, naive, tautologous—all which, though charming to us as indications of the antiquity of the poem, are not to be regarded as poetical excellencies. The merits of Homer's style, if we make due allowance for the wonderful language he had to wield, are the merits which all early poets, in some degree possess; and its faults, if we dare call them so, are likewise the faults of early poets. In fact, the style is not an elaborate—not a cultivated—not an artistic style.

"Grote's History of Greece: The Homeric Poems," *Westminster Review,* XLVI (1846), 408–412.

---

[4] Robert Montgomery (1807–1855); August Heinrich (Hoffmann von Fallersleben) (1798–1874).

Goethe

* * * Let me at once say that Goethe belonged to the *objective* class. * * * In every passage of his works may be read a strong feeling for the real, the concrete, the living; and a repugnance as strong for the vague, the abstract, or the supersensuous. His constant striving was to study Nature, so as to see her *directly*, and not through the mists of fancy, or through the distortions of prejudice—to look at men, and into them—to apprehend things as they were. In his conception of the universe he could not separate God *from* it, placing God above it, beyond it, as the philosophers did who represented God whirling the universe round his finger, "seeing it go." Such a conception revolted him. He animated the universe with God; he animated fact with divine life; he saw in Reality the incarnation of the Ideal; he saw in Morality the high and harmonious action of all human tendencies; he saw in Art the highest representation of Life. Nature, Nature, Nature is everywhere the burden of his striving. * * * To overlook and undervalue the facts of Nature, and to fix attention on fleeting personal impressions, or purely individual fancies, was a sign of decadence at every period of history. * * * His vision was all directed outwards. If we look through his works with critical attention, we shall observe the objective tendency determining—first, his choice of subjects; secondly, his handling of character; and, thirdly, his style. Intimately connected with this concreteness is another characteristic of his genius. His imagination was not, like that of many poets, incessantly at work in the combination and recombination of images which could be accepted for their own sake. It demanded the confrontation with fact; it moved with ease only on the secure ground of Reality. In science there are men whose active imaginations carry them into hypothesis and speculation, all the more easily because they do not bring hypothesis to the stern test of fact. The mere delight in combining ideas suffices them: provided the deductions are *log-ical*, they seem almost indifferent to their *truth*. There are poets of this order; indeed most poets are of this order. Goethe was of a quite opposite tendency. In him an imperious desire for reality controlled the errant facility of imagination. "The first and last thing demanded of Genius," he says, "is love of truth."[1]

Hence we see why he was led to portray men and women instead of demigods and angels: no Posas and Theklas, but Egmonts and Clärchens. Hence also his portraitures carry their moral *with* them, *in* them, but have no moral superposed,—no accompanying verdict as from some outside judge. His drama is without a chorus. Further,—and this is a point to be insisted on,—his style, both in poetry and prose, is subject to the same law. It is vivid with pictures, but it has scarcely any extraneous imagery. Most poets describe objects by metaphors or comparisons; Goethe seldom tells you what an object is *like*, he tells you what it *is*. Shakespeare is very unlike Goethe in this respect. The prodigal luxuriance of his imagery often entangles, in its overgrowth, the movement of his verse. It is true, he also is eminently concrete; he sees the real object vividly, and he makes us see it vividly; but he scarcely ever paints it save in the colours of metaphor and simile. Shakespeare's imagery bubbles up like a perpetual spring: to say that it repeatedly *overflows*, is only to say that his mind was lured by its own sirens away from the direct path. He did not master his Pegasus at all times, but let the wild careering creature take its winged way. Goethe, on the contrary, always masters his: perhaps because his steed had less of restive life in its veins. Not only does he master it, and ride with calm assured grace, he seems so bent on reaching the goal, that he scarcely thinks of anything else. To quit metaphor, he may be said to use with the utmost sparingness all the extraneous aids of imagery; he tries to create images of the objects, rather than other images of what the objects are like.

[1] "Das Erste und Letzte, was von Genie gefordert wird, ist Wahrheitsliebe." Goethe's *Maximen und Reflexionen* in *Goethe Werke* (Berlin: Paul Stapf, 1962), I, 1202.

Shakespeare, like Goethe, was a decided realist. He, too, was content to let his pictures of life carry their own moral with them. He uttered no moral verdict; he was no Chorus preaching on the text of what was pictured. Hence we cannot gather from his works what were his opinions. But there is this difference between him and Goethe, that his intense sympathy with the energetic passions and fierce volitions of our race made him delight in heroic characters, in men of robust frames and impassioned lives. Goethe, with an infusion of the best blood of Schiller, would have been a Shakespeare; but, such as Nature made him he was—Goethe, not Shakespeare.

THE SECOND PART OF FAUST

In the presence of this poem, I feel more embarrassment than with any other of Goethe's works. Difficult as the task has been in each instance to convey an adequate idea of the work before me, and to give expression to the opinion formed respecting it, that difficulty becomes complicated in the present instance by the consciousness of the opposition existing between a certain class of admirers and myself, a class not of ignorant, prejudiced, but of enlightened and ingenious intellects. These admirers speak of the *Second Part of Faust* as a work of transcendent merit, surpassing all that Goethe has written, a storehouse of profound and mystic philosophy, a miracle of execution. Others again, and these among Goethe's most loving students, declare it to be of mediocre interest, very far inferior to the *First Part,* and both in conception and execution an elaborate mistake. And of these I am one. I have tried to understand the work; tried to place myself at the right point of view for perfect enjoyment; but repeated trials, instead of clearing up obscurities and deepening enjoyment, as with the other works, have more and more confirmed my first impressions. Now although it needs but little experience to suggest that the fault may be wholly mine * * * nevertheless I must express my real convictions, and not withhold them on the chance that future enlightenment may cause me to alter them. What Channing says of opinions generally, is applicable to critical opinions: we are answerable for their uprightness, not for their *rightness*.[2]

Moreover, comparing the impressions produced by *Faust* and by the *Second Part*, although it is true that in both cases a sense of disappointment is created, the kind of objection made to each is entirely different. In *Faust*, a want of familiarity with the work may cause it to appear fragmentary, discordant, irreverent, not sufficiently metaphysical and so forth; but a single reading is enough to impress us with a sense of its interest, its pathos, its poetry, its strongly-marked character. In other words, the substance of the work lays hold of us; it is only the execution upon which criticism exercises itself. If we think it fragmentary, the fragments are at any rate of deep significance. If we think it deficient in taste, we never reproach it with want of power. The reverse is the case with this *Second Part*. Our objections are not raised by the details, but by the body of the poem; it is not the execution, but the whole conception, both in respect to the story itself, and to the mode of working out that story. What is the consequence? The consequence is that familiarity with *Faust* removes our objections and intensifies our admiration; but familiarity with the *Second Part* confirms our objections, and discloses their source.

If we remember that all Goethe's works are biographical, are parts of his life, and expressions of the various experiences he underwent, and the various stages of culture he passed through, there will be a peculiar interest in examining this product of his old age. * * * Taking up the biographical clue, we have seen in previous chapters the gradual development of a tendency towards mysticism and over-reflectiveness, which, visible as a germ in his earliest years, grew with his growth, and expanded in the later years, till its overgrowth shadowed and perplexed his more vigorous concrete tendencies, and made this clearest and most spontaneous of poets as fond of symbols as if he had

[2] See William Ellery Channing, "The System of Exclusion and Denunciation in Religion Considered," [1815] *The Works of William Ellery Channing* (Boston, 1899), pp. 478 ff.

been a priest of Isis. To those—and they are many—who think the aim and purpose of Art is to create symbols for Philosophy, this development will be prized as true progress. Others who do not thus subordinate the artist to the thinker, must regard the encroachment of Reflection as a sign of decay. It is quite true that Modern Art, as representative of the complexity of Modern Life, demands a large admixture of Reflection; but the predominance of the reflective tendency is a sign of decay. It is true that for an organism of a certain degree of complexity, an internal osseous structure is necessary; but the increase of ossification is cause and consequence of decay of vital power.

   * * * If the artist desires to express certain philosophic conceptions by means of symbols, he must never forget that, Art being Representation, the symbols chosen must possess *in themselves* a charm independent of what they mean. The forms which are his materials, the symbols which are his language, must in themselves have a beauty, and an interest, readily appreciable by those who do not understand the occult meaning. Unless they have this they cease to be Art; they become hieroglyphs. Art is picture-painting, not picture-writing. Beethoven, in his Symphonies, may have expressed grand psychological conceptions, which, for the mind that interprets them, may give them an extra charm; but if the strains in themselves do not possess a magic, if they did not sting the soul with a keen delight, then let the meaning be ever so profound, it will pass unheeded, because the *primary requisite* of music is not that it shall present grand thoughts, but that it shall agitate the audience with musical emotions. The poet who has only profound meanings, and not the witchery which is to carry his expression of those meanings home to our hearts, has failed. The primary requisite of poetry is that it shall move us; not that it shall instruct us.

   The Second Part of Faust, if the foregoing be correct, is a failure, because it fails in the primary requisite of a poem. Whatever else it may be, no one will say it is moving. The scenes, incidents, and characters do not *in themselves* carry that overpowering charm which masters us in the *First Part.* They borrow their interest from the meanings they are supposed to symbolize. Only in proportion to your ingenuity in guessing the riddle is your interest excited by the means. Mephisto, formerly so marvellous a creation, has become a mere mouthpiece; Faust has lost all traces of humanity, every pulse of emotion. The philosophic critics will point out how this change is necessary, because in the *Second Part* all that was individual has become universal. But this is only a description, not a justification; it is dignifying failure with a philosophic purpose. * * * To conduct *Faust* into a higher region it was not necessary to displace the struggles of an individual by representative abstractions; above all, it was not necessary to forsake the real domain of Art for that of Philosophy, and sacrifice beauty to meaning. The defect of this poem does not lie in its occult meanings, but in the poverty of the life which those meanings are meant to animate. No matter how occult the meaning, so that the picture be fine. A lion may be the symbol of wakefulness, of strength, of kingliness, of solitariness, and of many other things, according to the arbitrary fancy of the artist; and it matters comparatively little whether we rightly or wrongly interpret the artist's meaning; but his lion must be finely executed, must excite our admiration *as* a lion, if we are to consider it a work of Art.

Respecting the philosophic meaning of the *First Part* critics battle, and will battle perhaps for ever; but they are tolerably unanimous respecting its beauty. The passions, poetry, sarcasm, fancy, wisdom, and thrilling thoughts as from some higher world; the pathos and naïveté of Gretchen; the cruel coldness of Mephisto; the anguish of the restless student; these are what all understand, and understanding, enjoy. We may baffle ourselves with the mystery; we all are enchanted with the picture. We are moved by it as children are moved while reading the *Pilgrim's Progress*, believing all its allegorical persons and incidents to be real. When the child grows older, and learns to read beneath the allegory a series of grand representative abstractions, a new enjoyment is added; but even then the enjoyment depends less on the meaning than on the form. In all attempts at allegory which make the meaning prominent, and neglect the form, the effect is cold, lifeless, uninteresting. Allegory, which has been said to tell the story of a mind while seeming to tell the story of a life, is only acceptable on the condition of its story being interesting in itself. *The Second Part of Faust* fails in this first requisite. You must have the key to it. There is no direct appeal to the emotions. There is no intrinsic beauty in the symbols. In saying this I speak of it as a whole; there are many passages of exquisite beauty, some lines of profound thought, and some happy sarcasm; but there is no incident, no character, no one scene which lives in the memory like the incidents, characters, and scenes of the *First Part*.

The Life of Goethe (3rd ed.; London: Smith, Elder, 1875), pp. 52–54, 548–551.

Percy Bysshe Shelley

That Shelley "wailed" it is true, but so did Luther, at the errors he saw around him, and it is a mistake to say Shelley was "always wailing;" there is more love, and hope, and gladness, and delight in beauty and nature, in his poems, than in almost any other poet. Carlyle, speaking of Johnson, said, "If he had been asked to be Lord Chancellor, he would have felt uneasy at the great weight to be put on his shoulders. What did he care for riding in gilt coaches from Westminster to Whitehall? But had you told him that by his individual endeavour he could have benefited mankind, the unquenchable energy of the man would have arisen, and he would have shrunk from no toil, no obloquy, no misery, to attain it." We quote from memory (out of his eloquent Lectures on "Heroes and Hero-worship" delivered last May). Now we say, precisely was this Shelley's case; he refused all the paltry ambition of "gilt coaches" and "seats in Parliament," but he devoted himself to the cause of mankind, and through sickness and through sorrow, through obloquy and inhuman tyranny, through almost universal execration and obstacle, the firm heroic spirit of the man passed on, arrayed in the panoply of his own strong conscience, of his indestructible faith in truth and earnestness, and filled the world with wailings of the misery and corruption of the present state of things, and with psalm-music breaking forth into peals of holiest awe at the divine majesty of nature, or wild pæans of hope at the coming future.

However, as we said, the opinion that he was the memorable man of his day is getting itself settled in higher quarters. In the meanwhile, let us take a glance at his poetical works.

When Solon was asked if he had given his countrymen the best laws, he answered, the "best they are capable of receiving."[1] This appears to us to be one of the profoundest utterances on

---

[1] Plutarch's *Lives*, "Solon: Lawgiver."

record, and yet, as with all great truths, so simple that it is rarely comprehended; it contains, as we think, the whole philosophy of history; it utters a truth which, had it been recognized, would have saved men an immensity of vain, idle dispute, and would have led them into the clearer paths of knowledge of the past. It means this: that all truths are *truths of periods*, and not truths for eternity. That whatever great fact has had strength and vitality enough to realize itself, whether of religion, morals, government, &c., and to find place in this world, has been a truth for the time, and as good as men were "capable of receiving." To impose ideal truth, or law, upon an incapable, real man, must ever be a vain and empty speculation. The Old Testament, for example, contained a truth fitting to be received by the Hebrews of the time; but as the world progressed it became *unfitting*, and a New Testament arose. Catholicism was a vital truth in its earliest ages, but it became obsolete, and Protestantism arose. Suppose you were to preach to a band of red Indians the doctrines of Christ, what would they make of it? Would it not be necessary first to instil some general principles into them, to give them a *part* of Christianity, and so gradually fit them for the reception of the whole? It is with the growth of the world as with the growth of man, that "microcosm of the world." In babyhood he must have long clothes, be fed on succulent pap, and be dependent on nurses (commonly of the priest order). But the child grows, gets restive, and thinks it could dispense with long clothes and pap, and take to petticoats and stronger food. It grows still, and gets into jacket and trousers; and finally outgrowing these, demands coat and Wellingtons, with liberty to choose its own food and its own amusements and doings. Now if an ambitious mother insist on clothing her newly presented infant in the garments of manhood, allowing it also the choice of food and of action as in manhood, the result may be foreseen. If, on the other hand, she be a timid and unwise mother, and endeavour to keep it in swaddling clothes and feed it on pap all its life, the consequence may be foreseen to be rebellion and contention on the part of the child, with forcible seizure of man's garments; this is the error of Toryism, it would keep the world in long clothes.

Man's large "Discourse of (Un)-Reason," however, has always been of the timid mother kind, and not seeing that its child has outgrown its clothes, needing more fitting ones, there has always been a huge struggle on the part of the child and forcible seizure, named revolutions. Now here we come to the distinctive position of the poet. He is, as we before said, ever the first reformer; he sees that the world's present clothes have become too small for it, and it needs others. To proclaim this is his mission. If he does not see such a condition, but only fancies it, then is his proclamation unheeded; but if he really see it, and thus utters the indistinct thought of the masses, he becomes the great teacher of his age, giving articulate utterance to the inarticulate yearnings, feelings, wants of his brethren; embodying their tendencies, mirroring all and mirrored in all the age produces. This one great fact is the primal feature of his poetic existence, and from its central fire irradiates every dim cell of his mind. * * *

Shelley does not so much preach as inspire. He knew that it is not what we absolutely learn and can carry away with us, but what we *become,* which the poet's works effect. The French Revolution was the proclamation written in blood, that the world had outgrown its clothes, and would have others. England followed, and in that turbulent period there arose a band of poets to utter the new doctrines, such as will never pass out of literature. But let us look at their positions. They all saw that the existing state of things was corrupt—how far did they tend towards its alleviation? Scott resorted to the past, called up the dead spirit of chivalry before our eyes, and passed in panoramic manner the whole bygone days, with their border forays, pageants, tourneys, merrymen of the forest, brawny fighters clad in buff and steel, quick-blooded, vigorous-fibred men * * * performing prodigies of valour, living in the wild eddies of danger, beacon-lighted by war and intrigue. But it was the dead past, and bore in its womb no living future. Wordsworth, Southey, and Coleridge—these men began life with their wild youthful theories of Pantisocracy, but they all three started back at the apparition of Liberty they had called up; in neither of them lay the heroic endurance to carry out at all costs the gospel they had received, and so we find them all three resorting to other worlds than the present. Wordsworth, to an impossible state of country life or nature—hymning nature as the only healthy nurse, but stopping short whenever he came to any important point. Southey (of whom this present reviewer, having never read his poetry, will prefer silence), we see altogether choosing foreign and past scenes, Madoes, Rodericks, Thalabas, etc. Coleridge, also dreaming in the slumbers of the past, but unsettled, remote, altogether vague and intangible. Byron mirroring the disease of the age—the disease of unbelief and self-anatomy * * * talking about liberty, but the next moment laughing and mocking it and all things—he was no "spiritual leader of his people" to any goal of happiness or wisdom. Moore, bursting lyrically out into occasional nationalism, but in all his larger works seeking the remote past—orientalism, voluptuousness, nature's beauty, etc. *but no Gospel.* Keats, remote and unsettled, seeing much that was wrong, but not clearly seeing where and how it could be righted. Leigh Hunt, seeing the disease, and devoting himself with heroic endurance to the cure—but this as a philosopher—as a poet merely girding at conventional morals, and trying to bring round broader and truer ones.

Shelley alone was the poet standing completely on his truth; giving up his life to it, and eternally preaching it. Look where you will throughout his various works, there you see this gospel ever lying underneath, even under the smallest poems. It stands written there, unchangeable as the word in a firework illumination remains burning visible through all the varieties of fire which play around it and from out of it. One may see also from this why these other men, mirroring, as they did, the immediate restlessness and disease of the period, were more *notable* than this other man who was speaking of futurity in which he could be joined but by the minority; but his fame has been rapidly widening as the morn since his death, and has not yet nearly attained its culminating point.

The vital truth Shelley everywhere enforced, although treated as a chimera by most of his contemporaries, and indulged as a dream by some others, has become the dominant Idea—the philosophy and faith of this age, throughout Europe—it is progression, humanity, perfectability, civilization, democracy—call it what you will—this is the truth uttered unceasingly by Shelley, and universally received by us. It is easy to laugh at the "doctrine of perfectibility," and by grave sneers conceive that we annihilate it; but is that imperfect outlooking of the projective sympathy with humanity truly but a dream? If the data assumed are questionable, what are the data against it? Moreover, note this much of practical, present truth in it—it is the goal, admitted or not, of every human energy! * * * Why must we needs daily fight the desperate but irresistible battle of improvement, but that we have all, lying down in the dim souls of the meanest of us, however obscured by errors and worldly shows, some pregnant Idea tantamount to this doctrine of perfectibility, some religious Idea, which we indefinitely seek to realize, if not for ourselves at least for our children, and exhort them to do the same? When is this to stop? Or will it be answered, "It will never stop; it is the restless spirit of man impelling him from within." Good! now answer this: "* * * Is there no advancement for man, only a restless whirling round in a circle, like a blind horse in a mill? Is the past and present history of man a mere bubble—"a tale told by an idiot, full of sound and fury signifying nothing;" or is rather man's life and endeavour a stammering and confused utterance of eternal truth?" According to these two views will be your opinion of Shelley.

Thus much concerning the deeper significance of his condition as a poet. Of his claims as an artist we do not think so highly, for although not one of his contemporaries has produced a single work equal to *The Cenci,* yet in the artistic parts Shelley was not so great.[2] He had a most marvellous command of language, music, and imagery, but in most of his larger poems there is too much glare and brilliancy—there is a want of proper "keeping"—of light and shade; he does not sufficiently subdue his

[2] See also G. H. Lewes' "Shelley and the Letters of Poets," *Westminster Review,* LVII (1852), 509: "Of all his contemporaries Shelley seems to us to have been the nearest approach in life and works to the ideal of a poet; we do not say he was the greatest, but he was the purest poet."

"tones" (to finish this painter's language) so as to produce the essential harmony of colouring. He is too remote—too fond of talking about "eyes drinking being" from the form of a beloved. To illustrate this, he sometimes uses the epithet *"wingless* boat." A prosaic critic would say that boats not usually having wings, to call one wingless is superfluous; and although the prosaic critic would thereby prove himself, as he always does, to be a discoverer of mares' nests, and one might ask him if Shelley did not know that as well as he, yet his objection to the epithet would be well founded, though ill expressed. By "wingless" the student of Shelley knows that he means to intimate extreme swiftness by some supernatural means, but this meaning is too remote for poetry. Further, one may note a certain want of *objectivity*—a want of plastic powers in his descriptions; you can never identify them— they seem rather to have been broken memories of many a scene woven into one than the description of any particular scene. It has the effect of dreaminess—as one who has basked in the sun with his eyes closed in some lovely spot, and on opening them looks around and all seems unreal; a dim, dreamy haze is spread between the scene and him. We should characterize his mind as sensitive and reflective, rather than plastic and creative. These are artistic faults which must be taken into the scale while instituting a comparison with his contemporaries.

"Percy Bysshe Shelley," *Westminster Review,* XXXV (1841), 317–322.

Wordsworth's *Prelude*

Under any but the lowest aspect, that of mere curiosity, this poem must be regarded as an uninteresting performance, and an ambitious failure. We know that terrified critics (terrified lest they should be suspected of imperfect poetical taste if they talk not grandiloquently of Wordsworth) have agreed to rhapsodize its glories—the *Athenaeum* standing alone in withholding eulogies, and in quietly indicating its mediocre admiration of the work,[1] yet our purpose being not to flatter the prejudices of any class, but to express opinions whatever amount of opposition they may excite, we do not hesitate to affirm the poem to be a failure. As an autobiography it is meagre and futile beyond anything of a biographical kind we have seen; as a philosophical survey of the genesis of a poet's mind it fails in distinctness, in grasp, in coherence, and in introspective analysis: the utmost that can be said is that here is a collection of anecdotes, mostly trivial, regarding his early life, gathered together without any artistic sense of coordination or mutual irradiation, and written in a style sometimes lofty, picturesque, and instinct with poetry, but often surcharged with a dense prosaism to be paralleled only by passages from his other works. * * *

On matters of taste differences are admissible,—there is no arguing against feeling. But on matters of philosophy—if anywhere—reason asserts her claim, and brings forth demonstrations to support it. There is a notion current in the vague talk of the day that Wordsworth is a great *philosophical poet*—a notion we hold to be demonstrably incorrect. People here confound the *meditative, contemplative* spirit of Wordsworth with the creative, ratiocinative spirit of a philosophical poet, as seen in Sophocles, Lucretius, Shakespeare, Dante, Goethe, and others. Take any test of philosophy you please, and Wordsworth will be found

[1] *The Athenaeum,* August 3, 1850, p. 805.

wanting. * * * He does not grasp great truths and *illustrate* them (to employ the word in its primitive sense of purification). He does not form great conceptions and fill up the outlines with impassioned experience, in typical Events and Characters, or in great Representative abstractions. Two of his dominant qualities, closely allied, prevent any grandeur of conception, or of evolution, viz., *picturesqueness* and *triviality*; these lead him away from what is essential and typical to that which is accidental and particular.

Accordingly, although his works are full of picturesque details, they have little that is grand in them except the aspects of landscape nature, and little that is universally true except the reflections of his own personality. But in as much as nature appeals to all minds, and his diffusive egotism meets with responsive feelings, Wordsworth takes possession of us. There lies his strength. He is the greatest descriptive poet who ever lived. He is the greatest egotist who ever lived.[2] But he is not a philosophical poet in any exact meaning of the term. Want of human sympathy and an incurable bias towards the trivial, prevent his taking his place among the Shakespeares, Miltons, Dantes, and Goethes. In him it is the meanest flower that stirs his thoughts too deep for tears—the meanest flower, never the noblest Life! * * * What is *human* interests him only in as far as it is *picturesque*; and he avoids the great theatre whereon the tragic passions and exalted heroisms are displayed, to throw his whole poetic sympathy upon parochial woes! * * *

The reader will not, it is hoped, so far misconceive the drift of these remarks as to suppose us insensible to the depth of feeling, the brooding solemnity of thought, and the musical loveliness of imagery and diction which can be found scattered through Wordsworth's works. As a man forever communing with nature and with his own soul, and producing poetry unique in our literature, we assent to the highest claim set up for him; but as a philosophic poet, we unhesitatingly pronounce him mediocrity itself. * * *

[2] See *The Leader*, August 24, 1850, pp. 519–520, for an interesting example of Lewes' lack of dogmatism.

The Prelude, it would be easy to show, fails in every requisite of a philosophical exposition, and conception of what it purposes to be, viz., the genesis of a poet's mind. Only those unaccustomed to analysis, or unable to read beneath the efflorescence of imagery the substantial meaning forming the organic structure of a poem, can be deluded for an instant. * * *

The book entitled "Love of Nature leading to love of Man," may be said to resume the cardinal points of his philosophy, which is nothing else than the wretched absurdity that man, to keep himself pure and pious, should shun cities and the haunts of men, to shut himself in mountain solitudes. * * * Thus, if men are sunk in apathy and indifference, your task is not to re-awaken the great enthusiasms which once animate them, nor to withdraw the veil from those awful forms of Truth and Justice which dwell in every heart as in a temple; no, you must leave them to their apathy, and learn from sounding cataracts and winding mists all the lofty speculations that may secure your own salvation!

In this eighth Book he plainly states—that which we indeed knew before—how human beings first became interesting to him when he learned to look at them as *picturesque!* He loved them something better than his dog, a little less than the rocks and sounding cataracts. * * * Throughout this retrospect of a life he never softens with one deeply-felt affection, never hints that any one human being profoundly mingled with his life, modifying it, directing it, strengthening it! A few bald lines record that Calvert gave him independence—but there are no lines tremulous with tenderness towards any human being save his sister! With all this tenderness for Nature not a heart-beat for Man! As in Turner's pictures the pencil lingers fondly over water, skies, atmosphere, or light, while a few hasty indistinct scratches are given to the human figures, so in Wordsworth, Landscape Nature absorbs Human Nature. * * *

The feelings with which men regard Nature, as the symbolic reflection of human emotions or as the language in which God delivers himself to men, the whole range of sentiment, in short, which in modern poetry relates to Nature, was unknown to the ancients, as Schiller (in his "Essay on Naive and Sentimental Poetry") and subsequently Humboldt (in "Cosmos") have abundantly proved. Landscape, with ancient poets as well as with early painters, formed but the background for humanity. In the moderns this background has gradually assumed a greater and greater encroachment upon the foreground, till, in Wordsworth, it has completely *inverted* the ancient order. This is not a healthy symptom in art. Whenever accessories become elevated into principals, it is a sign of a false estimate of art; and this is the invariable tendency of inferior artists. Thus we see in German musicians harmony and orchestral effects predominating over melody and dramatic effects and although no one will deny the increased power of modern poetry derived from its saturation with this sentiment of nature's grandeur and loveliness, yet, after all, the Human Soul must ever remain the chief object of Art, and Nature itself only become interesting in as far as it is associated with man. To recur to our musical illustration, let us compare the introduction of the sentiment for nature, in its profound modification of our poetry, to the introduction of moving basses made by Carissimi,[3] whereby the domain of musical expression was so inexpressibly enlarged; without the moving bass what stupendous choral and orchestral effects would have been undreamt of, what gloom and grandeur uncreated. Nevertheless, to give predominance to moving basses over melodies would be to destroy music: and something of that error is committed by Wordsworth; but he is preserved from its full consequences by his own intense personality, which is always present to us and keeps up our interest, and by our own associations of personal experience with the phenomena he describes.

The Leader, August 17, 1850, pp. 496–497.

---

[3] Giacomo Carissimi (1605–1674), Italian composer and teacher.

Matthew Arnold

Scorn of the past we hold to be as unwise as scorn of "our wondrous Mother-Age"; but with whatever reverence and retrospective longing the Past is regarded, it should always be regarded as *past*: it should have historical, not absolute significance: it is our Ancestry, and not our Life. And as the retention in our organism of the elements which *have lived* is in itself a fatal source of destruction, poisoning the very life these elements once served, so in the onward progression of Humanity the old elements must pass away, transmitting to successors the work they had to perform:

And they finish their course and die.[1]

Matthew Arnold, in the Preface to this new edition of his poems [1853], defends himself against those critics who bid him "leave the exhausted past, and fix his thoughts upon the present." It seems to him that his critics know very little of what they are talking about. Whatever he may once have thought of "Our Age," it is clear he does not now regard it as so fruitful in poetry as the olden time; and all he says on this point is worthy of attention. * * *

But when he lays it down as a canon that the "highest problem of an art is to imitate actions," he seems to us either to employ an abusive extension of the term "action," or else to misconceive the problem and the function of Art. Indeed, one may say that Art is only an imitation of actions in its earliest and rudest forms. He himself is forced to admit that according to this canon *Faust* is not a great work of Art. * * *

[1] "Et quasi cursores vitai lampada tradunt." Lucretius, *De Rerum Natura*, Bk. 2, l. 79. It literally means, "And like runners through life they hand the torch," an expression referring to the Greek torch race in which runners kept torches burning and handed them on lighted.

A canon which excludes *Faust*, must *ipso facto* be suspicious. But Mr. Arnold's friends, the Ancients, will also fare badly if this rule be applied to them; even among the dramatists, in spite of action being the *principium et fons* of the drama, one meets with a Philoctetes for example, of which no one will say that the interest or beauty lies in the action; and if we turn to the *Divine Comedy* we shall find it as defective as *Faust* according to this rule. Actions are not ends in Art, but means to an end; they are not for their own sake, but for the sake of the thoughts and emotions they excite in us. Admirable as means, they are still only means. If the poet can reach his end through other means we do not tell him he has sinned against Art. * * *

Study the Classics, and beware of the syren-charms which enervate the Moderns! that is the text from which Arnold preaches. The logical consequence is Imitation.

Study the Classics and the Moderns too, but beware of the rudeness and baldness of the one, no less than of the rhetoric and glitter of the other! That is our text. For we believe the Ancients to have had every virtue and every vice conspicuous in the Moderns, over and above the remoteness of their ideas and feelings, which to us moderns becomes a vice. When the classics are good, they are so by virtue of qualities essential in all excellent works of Art; when they are bad, which is mostly the case, they are so by vice of qualities noticeable in every age—rudeness, incongruity, untruth, greater regard for manner than for matter, and for the mere fopperies of manner. Homer, with all his fine qualities is as rude as hemp; Aeschylus is often as fantastic, obscure, and incongruous, and Virgil as feeble, affected, and unpictorial as the very worst specimens which can be selected from eminent poets of Modern times. To deny this would be to deny evidence. It is not the traditional belief, but it is a fact.

Such being our critical faith, instead of Imitation we counsel Emulation; instead of following the mere fashions of Greek Art, follow no fashions but those which bear the general verdict of your age, and while learning from the Greeks the lessons they and all great artists have to teach, beware, above all things of imitating them.

Mr. Arnold, as a scholar, and one of poetical tendencies rather than of poetical genius, a man of culture, reflection, and sensibility, but not forming one of that small band of Singers who "sing as the birds sing," naturally looks towards Greece for inspiration. His poems will delight scholars, who will with curious pleasure follow him in his undisguised imitations of works which long have been their ideals: they will note his curiosities of verse, and his Graecism of imagery. Nor will the larger public read without delight. Poems such as these are not common. Some of the qualities most easily appreciable these poems possess, and they will secure an audience. But the fit audience is that of the cultured few.

The Leader, November 26, 1853, p. 1146, and December 3, 1853, p. 1170.

IV.
REALISM AND THE ART OF THE NOVEL

Realism and Idealism

* * * A distinction is drawn between Art and Reality, and an antithesis established between Realism and Idealism which would never have gained acceptance had not men in general lost sight of the fact that Art is a Representation of Reality—a Representation which, inasmuch as it is not the thing itself, but only represents it, must necessarily be limited by the nature of its medium; the canvas of the painter, the marble of the sculptor, the chords of the musician, and the language of the writer, each bring with them peculiar laws; but while thus limited, while thus regulated by the necessities imposed on it by each medium of expression, Art always aims at the representation of Reality, *i.e.* of Truth; and no departure from truth is permissible, except such as inevitably lies in the nature of the medium itself. Realism is thus the basis of all Art, and its antithesis is not Idealism, but *Falsism.* When our painters represent peasants with regular features and irreproachable linen; when their milkmaids have the air of Keepsake beauties, whose costume is picturesque, and never old or dirty; when Hodge is made to speak refined sentiments in unexceptionable English, and children utter long speeches of religious and poetic enthusiasm; when the conversation of the parlour and drawing-room is a succession of philosophical remarks, expressed with great clearness and logic, an attempt is made to idealize, but the result is simple falsification and bad art. To misrepresent the forms of ordinary life is no less an offence than to misrepresent the forms of ideal life: a pug-nosed Apollo, or Jupiter in a great-coat, would not be more truly shocking to an artistic mind than are those senseless falsifications of nature into which incompetence is led under the pretence of idealizing, of "beautifying" nature. Either give us true peasants, or leave them untouched; either paint no drapery at all, or paint it with the utmost fidelity; either keep your people silent, or make them speak the idiom of their class.

Raphael's marvellous picture, the "Madonna di San Sisto," presents us with a perfect epitome of illustration. In the figures of the Pope and St. Barbara we have a real man and woman, one of them a portrait, and the other not elevated above sweet womanhood. Below, we have the two exquisite angel children, intensely childlike, yet something *more,* something which renders their wings congruous with our conception of them. In the never-to-be-forgotten divine babe, we have at once the intensest realism of presentation, with the highest idealism of conception: the attitude is at once grand, easy, and natural; the face is that of a child, but the child is divine: in those eyes, and on that brow, there is an indefinable something which, greater than the expression of the angels', grander than that of pope or saint, is, to all who see it, a perfect *truth*; we feel that humanity in its highest conceivable form is before us, and that to transcend such a form would be to lose sight of the *human* nature there represented. In the virgin mother, again, we have a real woman, such as the *campagna* of Rome will furnish every day, yet with eyes subdued to a consciousness of her divine mission. Here is a picture which from the first has enchained the hearts of men, which is assuredly in the highest sense ideal, and which is so because it is also in the highest sense real—a real man, a real woman, real angel-children, and a real Divine Child; the last a striking contrast to the ineffectual attempts of other painters to spiritualize and idealize the babe—attempts which represent no babe at all. Titian's unsurpassable head of Christ, in the famous "Christo del Moneta," if compared with all other heads by other painters, will likewise be found to have its profound significance and idealism in the wonderful reality of the presentation: the head is more intensely human than that of any other representation of Christ, but the humanity is such as accords with our highest conceptions.

We may now come to an understanding on the significance of the phrase Idealism in Art. Suppose two men equally gifted with the perceptive powers and technical skill necessary to the accurate representation of a village group, but the one to be gifted, over and above these qualities, with an emotional sensibility which leads him to sympathize intensely with the emotions playing amid that village group. Both will delight in the forms of external nature, both will lovingly depict the scene and scenery; but the second will not be satisfied therewith: his sympathy will lead him to express something of the emotional life of the group; the mother in his picture will not only hold her child in a graceful attitude, she will look at it with a mother's tenderness; the lovers will be tender; the old people venerable. Without once departing from strict reality, he will have thrown a sentiment into his group which every spectator will recognize as poetry. Is he not more *real* than a Teniers, who, admirable in externals, had little or no sympathy with the internal life, which, however, is as real as the other? But observe, the sentiment must be real, truly expressed as a sentiment, and as the sentiment of the very people represented; the tenderness of *Hodge* must not be that of *Romeo*, otherwise we shall have such maudlin as the "Last Appeal."[1] * * *

The novelist . . . expresses his mind in his novels, and according as his emotional sympathy is keen and active, according to his poetic disposition, will the choice and treatment of his subject be poetical: but it must always be real—true. If he select the incidents and characters of ordinary life, he must be rigidly bound down to accuracy in the presentation. He is at liberty to avoid such subjects, if he thinks them prosaic and uninteresting (which will mean that he does not feel their poetry and interest), but having chosen, he is not at liberty to falsify, under pretense of beautifying them; every departure from truth in motive, idiom, or probability, is, to that extent, a defect. His dressmaker must be a young woman who makes dresses, and not a sentimental "heroine," evangelical and consumptive; she may be consumptive, she may also be evangelical, for dressmakers are so sometimes, but she must be individually a dressmaker. So also the merchant must have an air of the counting-house, an ostler must smell of the stables. To *call* a man a merchant, and tell us of his counting-house, while for anything else we might suppose him to be a nobleman, or an uncle from India, is not Art, because it is not representation of reality. If the writer's knowledge or

---

[1] Painted in 1843 by Frank Stone (1800–1859).

sympathies do not lead him in the direction of ordinary life, if he can neither paint town nor country, let him take to the wide fields of History or Fancy. Even there the demands of truth will pursue him; he must paint what he distinctly *sees* with his imagination; if he succeed, he will create characters which are true although ideal; and in this sense Puck, Ariel, Brutus, and Falstaff are as real as Dick Swiveller or Tom Jones. * * *

"Realism in Art: Recent German Fiction," *Westminster Review*, LXX (1858), 493–496.

The Novels of Jane Austen

If, as probably few will dispute, the art of the novelist be the representation of human life by means of a story; and if the *truest* representation, effected by the *least expenditure* of means, constitutes the highest claim of art, then we say that Miss Austen has carried the art to a point of excellence surpassing that reached by any of her rivals. Observe we say "the art"; we do not say that she equals many of them in the *interest* excited by the art; that is a separate question. * * * Miss Austen has nothing fervid in her works. She is not capable of producing a profound agitation in the mind. In many respects this is a limitation of her powers, a deduction from her claims. But while other writers have had more power over the emotions, more vivid imaginations, deeper sensibilities, deeper insight, and more of what is properly called invention, no novelist has approached her in what we may style the "economy of art," by which is meant the easy adaptation of means to ends, with no aid from extraneous or superfluous elements. Indeed, paradoxical as the juxtaposition of the names may perhaps appear to those who have not reflected much on this subject, we venture to say that the only names we can place above Miss Austen, in respect of this economy of art, are Sophocles and Molière (in *Le Misanthrope*). And if anyone will examine the terms of the definition, he will perceive that almost all defects in works of art arise from neglect of this economy. When the *end* is the representation of human nature in its familiar aspects, moving amid every-day scenes, the *means* must likewise be furnished from every-day life: romance and improbabilities must be banished as rigorously as the grotesque exaggeration of peculiar characteristics, or the representation of abstract types. It is easy for the artist to choose a subject from every-day life, but it is not easy for him to so represent the characters and their actions that they shall be at once lifelike and interesting;

accordingly, whenever ordinary people are introduced, they are either made to speak a language never spoken out of books, and to pursue conduct never observed in life; or else they are intolerably wearisome. But Miss Austen is like Shakespeare: she makes her very noodles inexhaustibly amusing, yet accurately real. We never tire of her characters. They become equal to actual experiences. They live with us, and form perpetual topics of comment. * * *

The absence of breadth, picturesqueness, and passion will * * * limit the appreciating audience of Miss Austen to the small circle of cultivated minds; and even these minds are not always capable of greatly relishing her works. We have known very remarkable people who cared little for her pictures of every-day life; and indeed it may be anticipated that those who have little sense of humour, or whose passionate and insurgent activities demand in art a reflection of their own emotions and struggles, will find little pleasure in these homely comedies. Currer Bell may be taken as a type of these. She was utterly without a sense of humour, and was by nature fervid and impetuous. In a letter published in her memoirs she writes,—"Why do you like Miss Austen so very much? I am puzzled on that point * * * I had not read *Pride and Prejudice* till I read that sentence of yours, and then I got the book. And what did I find? An accurate daguerreotyped portrait of a commonplace face; a carefully-fenced, highly-cultivated garden, with neat borders and delicate flowers; but no glance of a bright, vivid physiognomy, no open country, no fresh air, no blue hill, no bonny beck. I should hardly like to live with her elegant ladies and gentlemen in their elegant but confined houses."[1] The critical reader will not fail to remark the almost contemptuous indifference to the art of truthful portrait-painting which this passage indicates; and he will understand, perhaps, how the writer of such a passage was herself incapable of drawing more than characteristics, even in her most

---

[1] For the story of Lewes' influence on Charlotte Brontë, see Clement Shorter (ed.), *The Brontës: Life and Letters* (London: Hodder and Stoughton, 1908), I, 364–368; and Franklin Gary, "Charlotte Brontë and George Henry Lewes," *PMLA*, LI (1936), 518–542.

successful efforts. Jane Eyre, Rochester, and Paul Emmanuel, are very vigorous sketches, but the reader observes them from the *outside*, he does not penetrate their souls, he does not know them. * * *

We acknowledge the great attractions which a novel may receive from the general vigour and culture of the author; and acknowledge that such attractions form but a very small element in Miss Austen's success. Her pages have no sudden illuminations. There are neither epigrams nor aphorisms, neither subtle analyses nor eloquent descriptions. She is without grace or felicity of expression; she has neither fervid nor philosophic comment. Her charm lies solely in the art of representing life and character, and that is exquisite.

Blackwood's, LXXXVI (1859), 101–109.

Dickens in Relation to Criticism

* * * Dickens has proved his power by a popularity almost unexampled, embracing all classes. Surely it is a task for criticism to exhibit the sources of that power? If everything that has ever been alleged against the works be admitted, there still remains an immense success to be accounted for. It was not by their defects that these works were carried over Europe and America. It was not their defects which made them the delight of grey heads on the bench, and the study of youngsters in the counting-house and school-room. Other writers have been exaggerated, untrue, fantastic, and melodramatic; but they have gained so little notice that no one thinks of pointing out their defects. It is clear, therefore, that Dickens had powers which enabled him to triumph in spite of the weaknesses which clogged them; and it is worth inquiring what those powers were, and their relation to his undeniable defects.

I am not about to attempt such an inquiry, but simply to indicate two or three general points of view. It will be enough merely to mention in passing the primary cause of his success, his overflowing fun, because even uncompromising opponents admit it. They may be ashamed of their laughter, but they laugh. A revulsion of feeling at the preposterousness or extravagance of the image may follow the burst of laughter, but the laughter is irresistible, whether rational or not, and there is no arguing away such a fact.

Great as Dickens is in fun, so great that Fielding and Smollett are small in comparison, he would have been only a passing amusement for the world had he not been gifted with an imagination of marvellous vividness, and an emotional, sympathetic nature capable of furnishing that imagination with elements of universal power. Of him it may be said with less exaggeration than of most poets, that he was of "imagination all compact;" if the other higher faculties were singularly deficient in him, this faculty was imperial. He was a seer of visions; and his visions were of objects at once familiar and potent. Psychologists will understand both the extent and the limitation of the remark, when I say that in no other perfectly sane mind (Blake, I believe, was not perfectly sane) have I observed vividness of imagination approaching so closely to hallucination. Many who are not psychologists may have had some experience in themselves, or in others, of that abnormal condition in which a man hears voices, and sees objects, with the distinctness of direct perception, although silence and darkness are without him; these *revived* impressions, revived by an internal cause, have precisely the same force and clearness which the impressions originally had when produced by an external cause. In the same degree of vividness are the images *constructed* by his mind in explanation of the voices heard or objects seen: when he imagines that the voice proceeds from a personal friend, or from Satan tempting him, the friend or Satan stands before him with the distinctness of objective reality; when he imagines that he himself has been transformed into a bear, his hands are seen by him as paws. In vain you represent to him that the voices he hears have no external existence; he will answer, as a patient pertinently answered Lélut[1]: "You believe that I am speaking to you because you hear me, is it not so? Very well, I believe that voices are speaking to me because I hear them." There is no power of effacing such conviction by argument. You may get the patient to assent to any premises you please, he will not swerve from his conclusions. I once argued with a patient who believed he had been transformed into a bear; he was quite willing to admit that the idea of such a transformation was utterly at variance with all experience; but he always returned to his position that God being omnipotent there was no reason to doubt his power of transforming men into bears: what remained fixed in his mind was the image of himself under a bear's form.

The characteristic point in the hallucinations of the insane,

[1] Louis François Lélut (1804–1877), famous French physician who wrote works on phrenology.

that which distinguishes them from hallucinations equally vivid in the sane, is the coercion of the image in *suppressing comparison* and all control of experience. Belief always accompanies a vivid image, for a time; but in the sane this belief will not persist against rational control. If I see a stick partly under water, it is impossible for me not to have the same feeling which would be produced by a bent stick out of the water—if I see two plane images in the stereoscope, it is impossible not to have the feeling of seeing one solid object. But these beliefs are rapidly displaced by reference to experience. I know the stick is not bent, and that it will not appear bent when removed from the water. I know the seeming solid is not an object in relief, but two plane pictures. It is by similar focal adjustment of the mind that sane people know that their hallucinations are unreal. The images may have the vividness of real objects, but they have not the properties of real objects, they do not preserve consistent relations with other facts, they appear in contradiction to other beliefs. Thus if I see a black cat on the chair opposite, yet on my approaching the chair feel no soft object, and if my terrier on the hearthrug looking in the direction of the chair shows none of the well-known agitation which the sight of a cat produces, I conclude, in spite of its distinctness, that the image is an hallucination.[2]

Returning from this digression, let me say that I am very far indeed from wishing to imply any agreement in the common notion that "great wits to madness nearly are allied;"[3] on the contrary, my studies have led to the conviction that nothing is less like genius than insanity, although some men of genius have had occasional attacks; and further, that I have never observed any trace of the insane temperament in Dickens's works, or life, they being indeed singularly free even from the eccentricities which often accompany exceptional powers; nevertheless, with

[2] G. H. Lewes, *The Physiology of Common Life* (2 vols.; Leipzig: B. Tauchnitz, 1860), II, 256, 257–259; *Mind as a Function of the Organism* (London: H. Trübner, 1879), pp. 344–345.

[3] Lewes deals with this issue in "Great Wits, Mad Wits?" *Blackwood's*, LXXXVIII (1860), 302–311.

all due limitations, it is true that there is considerable light shed upon his works by the action of the imagination in hallucination. To him also *revived* images have the vividness of sensations; to him also *created* images have the coercive force of realities, excluding all control, all contradiction. What seems preposterous, impossible to us, seemed to him simple fact of observation. When he imagined a street, a house, a room, a figure, he saw it not in the vague schematic way of ordinary imagination, but in the sharp definition of actual perception, all the salient details obtruding themselves on his attention. He, seeing it thus vividly, made us also see it; and believing in its reality however fantastic, he communicated something of his belief to us. He presented it in such relief that we ceased to think of it as a picture. So definite and insistent was the image, that even while knowing it was false we could not help, for a moment, being affected, as it were, by his hallucination.

This glorious energy of imagination is that which Dickens had in common with all great writers. It was this which made him a creator, and made his creations universally intelligible, no matter how fantastic and unreal. His types established themselves in the public mind like personal experiences. Their falsity was unnoticed in the blaze of their illumination. Every humbug seemed a Pecksniff, every nurse a Gamp, every jovial improvident a Micawber, every stinted serving-wench a Marchioness. Universal experiences became individualized in these types; an image and a name were given, and the image was so suggestive that it seemed to *express* all that it was found to *recall,* and Dickens was held to have depicted what his readers supplied. Against such power criticism was almost idle. In vain critical reflection showed these figures to be merely masks,—not characters, but personified characteristics, caricatures and distortions of human nature,—the vividness of their presentation triumphed over reflection: their creator managed to communicate to the public his own unhesitating belief. Unreal and impossible as these types were, speaking a language never heard in life, moving like pieces of simple mechanism always in one way (instead of moving with the infinite fluctuations of organisms, incalculable yet intelligible, surprising yet familiar), these unreal figures affected the uncritical reader with the force of reality; and they did so in virtue of their embodiment of some real characteristic vividly presented. The imagination of the author laid hold of some well-marked physical trait, some peculiarity of aspect, speech, or manner which every one recognized at once; and the force with which this was presented made it occupy the mind to the exclusion of all critical doubts: only reflection could detect the incongruity. Think of what this implies! Think how little the mass of men are given to reflect on their impressions, and how their minds are for the most part occupied with sensations rather than ideas, and you will see why Dickens held an undisputed sway. Give a child a wooden horse, with hair for mane and tail, and wafer-spots for colouring, he will never be disturbed by the fact that this horse does not move its legs, but runs on wheels—the general suggestion suffices for his belief; and this wooden horse, which he can handle and draw, is believed in more than a pictured horse by a Wouvermanns [sic] or an Ansdell.[4] It may be said of Dickens's human figures that they too are wooden, and run on wheels; but these are details which scarcely disturb the belief of admirers. Just as the wooden horse is brought within the range of the child's emotions, and dramatizing tendencies, when he can handle and draw it, so Dickens's figures are brought within the range of the reader's interests, and receive from these interests a sudden illumination, when they are the puppets of a drama every incident of which appeals to the sympathies. With a fine felicity of instinct he seized upon situations having an irresistible hold over the domestic affections and ordinary sympathies. He spoke in the mother-tongue of the heart, and was always sure of ready listeners. He painted the life he knew, the life every one knew; for if the scenes and manners were unlike those we were familiar with, the feelings and motives, the joys and griefs, the mistakes and efforts of the actors were universal, and therefore universally intelligible; so that even critical spectators who complained that

    [4] Philip Wouverman (1619–1668), Dutch painter of hunting scenes; Richard Ansdell (1815–1885), English painter of sporting scenes.

these broadly painted pictures were artistic daubs, could not wholly resist their effective suggestiveness. He set in motion the secret springs of sympathy by touching the domestic affections. He painted nothing ideal, heroic; but all the resources of the bourgeois epic were in his grasp. The world of thought and passion lay beyond his horizon. But the joys and pains of childhood, the petty tyrannies of ignoble natures, the genial pleasantries of happy natures, the life of the poor, the struggles of the street and back parlour, the insolence of office, the sharp social contrasts, east-wind and Christmas jollity, hunger, misery, and hot punch—these he could deal with, so that we laughed and cried, were startled at the revelation of familiar facts hitherto unnoted, and felt our pulses quicken as we were hurried along with him in his fanciful flight.

Such were the sources of his power. To understand how it is that critics quite competent to recognize such power, and even so far amenable to it as to be moved and interested by the works in spite of all their drawbacks, should have forgotten this undenied power, and written or spoken of Dickens with mingled irritation and contempt, we must take into account two natural tendencies—the bias of opposition, and the bias of technical estimate.

The bias of opposition may be illustrated in a parallel case. Let us suppose a scientific book to be attracting the attention of Europe by the boldness, suggestiveness, and theoretic plausibility of its hypotheses; this work falls into the hands of a critic sufficiently grounded in the science treated to be aware that its writer, although gifted with great theoretic power and occasional insight into unexplored relations, is nevertheless pitiably ignorant of the elementary facts and principles of the science; the critic noticing the power, and the talent of lucid exposition, is yet perplexed and irritated at ignorance which is inexcusable, and a reckless twisting of known facts into impossible relations, which seems wilful; will he not pass from marvelling at this inextricable web of sense and nonsense, suggestive insight and mischievous error, so jumbled together that the combination of this sagacity with this glaring inefficiency is a paradox, and be driven by the anger

of opposition into an emphatic assertion that the belauded philosopher is a charlatan and an ignoramus? A chorus of admirers proclaims the author to be a great teacher, before whom all contemporaries must bow; and the critic observes this teacher on one page throwing out a striking hypothesis of some geometric relations in the planetary movements, and on another assuming that the hypothenuse is equal to its perpendicular and base, because the square of the hypothenuse is equal to the squares of its sides—in one chapter ridiculing the atomic theory, and in another arguing that carbonic acid is obtained from carbon and nitrogen —can this critic be expected to join in the chorus of admirers and will he not rather be exasperated into an opposition which will lead him to undervalue the undeniable qualities in his insistence on the undeniable defects?

Something like this is the feeling produced by Dickens's works in many cultivated and critical readers. They see there human character and ordinary events portrayed with a mingled verisimilitude and falsity altogether unexampled. The drawing is so vivid yet so incorrect, or else is so blurred and formless, with such excess of *effort* (as of a showman beating on the drum) that the doubt arises how an observer so remarkably keen could make observations so remarkably false, and miss such very obvious facts; how the rapid glance which could swoop down on a peculiarity with hawk-like precision, could overlook all that accompanied and was organically related to that peculiarity; how the eye for characteristics could be so blind to character, and the ear for dramatic idiom be so deaf to dramatic language; finally, how the writer's exquisite susceptibility to the grotesque could be insensible to the occasional grotesqueness of his own attitude. Michael Angelo is intelligible, and Giotto is intelligible; but a critic is nonplussed at finding the invention of Angelo with the drawing of Giotto. It is indeed surprising that Dickens should have observed man, and not been impressed with the fact that man is, in the words of Montaigne, *un être ondoyant et diverse.*[5]

[5] *Essais,* Bk. 1, chap. 1: "Certes, c'est un sujet merveilleusement vain, divers et ondoyant, que l'homme." (Montaigne's famous lines on man as a "vain, diverse and undulating being.")

And the critic is distressed to observe the substitution of mechanisms for minds, puppets for characters. It is needless to dwell on such monstrous failures as Mantalini, Rosa Dartle, Lady Dedlock, Esther Summerson, Mr. Dick, Arthur Gride, Edith Dombey, Mr. Carker—needless, because if one studies the successful figures one finds even in them only touches of verisimilitude. When one thinks of Macawber always presenting himself in the same situation, moved with the same springs, and uttering the same sounds, always confident on something turning up, always crushed and rebounding, always making punch—and his wife always declaring she will never part from him, always referring to his talents and her family—when one thinks of the "catchwords" personified as characters, one is reminded of the frogs whose brains have been taken out for physiological purposes, and whose actions henceforth want the distinctive peculiarity of organic action, that of fluctuating spontaneity. Place one of these brainless frogs on his back and he will at once recover the sitting posture; draw a leg from under him, and he will draw it back again; tickle or prick him and he will push away the object, or take *one* hop out of the way; stroke his back, and he will utter *one* croak. All these things resemble the actions of the unmutilated frog, but they differ in being *isolated* actions, and *always the same:* they are as uniform and calculable as the movements of a machine. The uninjured frog may or may not croak, may or may not hop away; the result is never calculable, and is rarely a single croak or a single hop. It is this complexity of the organism which Dickens wholly fails to conceive; his characters have nothing fluctuating and incalculable in them, even when they embody true observations; and very often they are creations so fantastic that one is at a loss to understand how he could, without hallucination, believe them to be like reality. There are dialogues bearing the traces of straining effort at effect, which in their incongruity painfully resemble the absurd and eager expositions which insane patients pour into the listener's ear when detailing their wrongs, or their schemes. Dickens once declared to me that every word said by his characters was distinctly *heard* by him; I was at first not a little puzzled to account for the fact that he could hear language so utterly unlike the language of real feeling, and not be aware of its preposterousness; but the surprise vanished when I thought of the phenomena of hallucination. And here it may be needful to remark in passing that it is not because the characters are badly drawn and their language unreal, that they are to be classed among the excesses of imagination; otherwise all the bad novelists and dramatists would be credited with that which they especially want—powerful imagination. His peculiarity is not the incorrectness of the drawing, but the vividness of the imagination which while rendering that incorrectness insensible to him, also renders it potent with multitudes of his fellowmen. For although his weakness comes from excess in one direction, the force which is in excess must not be overlooked; and it is overlooked or undervalued by critics who, with what I have called the bias of opposition, insist only on the weakness.

This leads me to the second point, the bias of technical estimate. The main purpose of Art is delight. Whatever influences may radiate from that centre,—and however it may elevate or modify,—the one primary condition of influence is stirred emotion. No Art can teach which does not move; no Art can move without teaching. Criticism has to consider Art under two aspects, that of emotional pleasure, and that of technical pleasure. We all—public and critics—are susceptible of the former, are capable of being moved, and are delighted with what stirs the emotions, filling the mind with images having emotional influence; but only the critics are much affected by technical skill, and the pleasure it creates. *What* is done, what is suggested, constitutes the first aspect; *how* it is done the second. We all delight in imitation, and in the skill which represents one object in another medium; but the refinements of skill can only be appreciated by study. To a savage there is so little suggestion of a human face and form in a painted portrait that it is not even recognized as the representation of a man; whereas the same savage would delight in a waxwork figure, or a wooden Scotchman at the door of a tobacconist. The educated eye sees exquisite skill in the portrait, a skill which gives exquisite delight; but this eye which traces and estimates the subtle effects of colour and distribution of light and shade in the portrait, turns with disgust from the wax figure, or the wooden Highlander. In the course of time the pleasure derived from the perception of difficulty overcome, leads to such a preponderance of the technical estimate, that the sweep of the brush, or the composition of lines, becomes of supreme importance, and the connoisseur no longer asks, What is painted? but How is it painted? The *what* may be a patch of meadow, the bend of a river, or a street boy munching bread and cheese, and yet give greater delight by its *how,* than another picture which represented the Andes, Niagara, or a Madonna and Child. When the critic observes technical skill in a picture, he pronounces the painter to be admirable, and is quite unmoved by any great subject badly painted. In like manner a great poet is estimated by the greatness of his execution of great conceptions, not by the greatness of his intention.

How easily the critic falls into the mistake of overvaluing technical skill, and not allowing for the primary condition, how easily he misjudges works by applying to them technical rules derived from the works of others, need not here be dwelt on. What I wish to indicate is the bias of technical estimate which, acting with that bias of opposition just noted, has caused the critics to overlook in Dickens the great artistic powers which are proved by his immense success; and to dwell only on those great artistic deficiencies which exclude him from the class of exquisite writers. He worked in delf, not in porcelain. But his prodigal imagination created in delf forms which delighted thousands. He only touched common life, but he touched it to "fine issues;" and since we are all susceptible of being moved by pictures of children in droll and pathetic situations, and by pictures of common suffering and common joy, any writer who can paint such pictures with sufficient skill to awaken these emotions is powerful in proportion to the emotion stirred. That Dickens had this skill is undisputed; and if critical reflection shows that the means he employs are not such as will satisfy the technical estimate, and consequently that the pictures will not move the cultivated mind, nor give it the deep content which perfect Art continues to create, making the work a "joy for ever," we must still remember that in the present state of Literature, with hundreds daily exerting their utmost efforts to paint such pictures, it requires prodigious force and rare skill to impress images that will stir the universal heart. Murders are perpetrated without stint, but the murder of Nancy is unforgettable. Children figure in numberless plays and novels, but the deaths of little Nell and little Paul were national griefs. Seduction is one of the commonest of tragedies, but the scene in Peggoty's boat-house burns itself into the memory. Captain Cuttle and Richard Swiveller, the Marchioness and Tilly Slowboy, Pecksniff and Micawber, Tiny Tim and Mrs. Gamp, may be imperfect presentations of human character, but they are types which no one can forget. Dr. Johnson explained the popularity of some writer by saying, "Sir, *his* nonsense suited *their* nonsense;"[6] let us add, "and his sense suited their sense," and it will explain the popularity of Dickens. Readers to whom all the refinements of Art and Literature are as meaningless hieroglyphs, were at once laid hold of by the reproduction of their own feelings, their own experiences, their own prejudices, in the irradiating splendour of his imagination; while readers whose cultivated sensibilities were alive to the most delicate and evanescent touches were, by virtue of their common nature, ready to be moved and delighted at his pictures and suggestions. The cultivated and uncultivated were affected by his admirable *mise en scène,* his fertile invention, his striking selection of incident, his intense vision of physical details. Only the cultivated who are made fastidious by cultivation paused to consider the pervading commonness of the works, and remarked that they are wholly without glimpses of a nobler life; and that the writer presents an almost unique example of a mind of singular force in which, so to speak, sensations never passed into ideas. Dickens sees and feels, but the logic of feeling seems the only logic he can manage. Thought is strangely absent from his works. I do not suppose a

[6] According to Horace Walpole, October 22, 1774, in *The Letters of Horace Walpole,* ed. P. Toynbee (16 vols.; Oxford: Clarendon Press, 1904), IX, 74, Charles II is supposed to have made this remark in reference to a famous popular preacher.

single thoughtful remark on life or character could be found throughout the twenty volumes. Not only is there a marked absence of the reflective tendency, but one sees no indication of the past life of humanity having ever occupied him; keenly as he observes the objects before him, he never connects his observations into a general expression, never seems interested in general relations of things. Compared with that of Fielding or Thackeray, his was merely an *animal* intelligence, *i.e.*, restricted to perceptions.[7] On this ground his early education was more fruitful and less injurious than it would have been to a nature constructed on a more reflective and intellectual type. It furnished him with rare and valuable experience, early developed his sympathies with the lowly and struggling, and did not starve any intellectual ambition. He never was and never would have been a student. * * *

Fortnightly Review, XVII (1872), 143–151.

[7] For Lewes' view of Dickens' intellectual acumen, see also *The Leader,* December 11, 1852, p. 1189; January 15, 1853, p. 64; February 5, 1853, pp. 137–138; March 26, 1853, pp. 303–306; September 3, 1853, p. 858; "Spontaneous Combustion," *Blackwood's,* LXXXIX (1861), 385–402. See G. H. Ford's discussion of Lewes' paper on Dickens in *Dickens and His Readers: Aspects of Novel Criticism since 1836* (Princeton: Princeton University Press, 1955), pp. 149–153.

Herman Melville—*The Whale: or Moby Dick*

Want of originality has long been the just and standing reproach to American literature; the best of its writers were but
second-hand Englishmen. Of late some have given evidence of
originality; not *absolute* originality, but such genuine outcoming
of the American intellect as can be safely called national. Edgar
Poe, Nathaniel Hawthorne, Herman Melville are assuredly no
British offshoots; nor is Emerson—the *German* American that he
is! The observer of this commencement of an American literature, properly so called, will notice as significant that these writers
have a wild and mystic love of the supersensual, peculiarly their
own. To move a horror skilfully, with something of the earnest
faith in the Unseen, and with weird imagery to shape these
Phantasms so vividly that the most incredulous mind is hushed,
absorbed—to do this no European pen has apparently any longer
the power—to do this American literature is without a rival.
What *romance* writer can be named with Hawthorne? Who
knows the terrors of the seas like Herman Melville?

The Whale—Melville's last book—is a strange, wild, weird
book, full of poetry and full of interest. To use a hackneyed
phrase, it is indeed "refreshing" to quit the old, wornout path-
ways of romance, and feel the sea breezes playing through our
hair, the salt spray dashing on our brows, as we do here. One
tires terribly of ballrooms, dinners, and the incidents of town
life! One never tires of Nature. And there is Nature here, though
the daring imagery often grows riotously extravagant.

Then the ghostly terrors which Herman Melville so skilfully
evokes, have a strange fascination. In vain Reason rebels. Imagination is absolute. Ordinary superstitions related by vulgar pens
have lost their power over all but the credulous; but Imagination
has a credulity of its own respondent to power. So it is with
Melville's superstitions: we believe in them imaginatively. * * *

The book is not a romance, nor a treatise on Cetology. It is something of both: a strange, wild work with the tangled overgrowth and luxuriant vegetation of American forests, not the trim orderliness of an English park. Criticism may pick many holes in this work; but no criticism will thwart its fascination.

The Leader, November 8, 1851, pp. 1067–1068.

V.

THE THEATER: ON ACTORS AND THE ART OF ACTING

On the Actor

With the best wishes in the world I cannot bring myself to place the actor on a level with the painter or the author. I cannot concede to the actor such a parity of intellectual greatness; while, at the same time, I am forced to remember that, with inferior abilities, he secures far greater reward, both of pudding and praise. It is not difficult to assign the causes of an actor's superior reward, both in noisy reputation and in solid guineas. He amuses. He amuses more than the most amusing author. And our luxuries always cost us more than our necessities. Taglioni or Carlotta were better paid than Edmund Kean or Macready; Jenny Lind[1] better than both put together. * * *

The truth is, we exaggerate the talent of an actor because we judge only from the effect he produces, without inquiring too curiously into the means. But, while the painter has nothing but his canvas and the author has nothing but white paper and printer's ink with which to produce his effects, the actor has all other arts as handmaids: the poet labors for him, creates his part, gives him his eloquence, his music, his imagery, his tenderness, his pathos, his sublimity; the scene-painter aids him; the costumes, the lights, the music, all the fascinations of the stage—all subserve the actor's effect: these raise him upon a pedestal; remove them, and what is he? He who can make a stage mob bend and sway with his eloquence, what could he do with a real mob, no poet by to prompt him? He who can charm us with the stateliest imagery of a noble mind, when robed in the sables of Hamlet, or in the toga of Coriolanus, what can he do in coat and trousers on the world's stage? Rub off the paint, and the eyes are no longer brilliant! Reduce the actor to his intrinsic value, and then weigh him with the rivals whom he surpasses in reputation and in fortune.

[1] Ballet dancers: Marie Taglioni (1804–1884), Carlotta Grisi (1821–1899); Actors: Edmund Kean (1787–1833), William Charles Macready (1793–1873); Singer: Jenny Lind (1820–1887).

If my estimate of the intrinsic value of acting is lower than seems generally current, it is from no desire to disparage an art I have always loved; but from a desire to state what seems to me the simple truth on the matter, and to show that the demand for posthumous fame is misplaced. Already the actor gets more fame than he deserves, and we are called upon to weep that he gets no more. During his reign the applause which follows him exceeds in intensity that of all other claimants for public approbation; so long as he lives he is an object of strong sympathy and interest; and when he dies he leaves behind him such influence upon his art as his genius may have effected (true fame!) and a monument to kindle the emulation of successors. * * * In this crowded world how few there are who can leave even a name, how rare those who leave more. The author can be read by future ages! Oh! yes, he *can* be read: the books are preserved; but *is* he read? Who disturbs them from their repose upon the dusty shelves of silent libraries? What are the great men of former ages, with rare, very rare, exceptions, but *names* to the world which shelves their well-bound volumes!

Unless some one will tell me in sober gravity (what is some-times absurdly said in fulsome dinner speeches and foolish dedi-cations) that the actor has a "kindred genius" with the poet, whose creations he represents, and that in sheer intellectual calibre Kean and Macready were nearly on a par with Shake-speare, I do not see what cause of complaint can exist in the actor's not sharing the posthumous fame of a Shakespeare. His fame while he lives surpasses that of almost all other men. Byron was not so widely worshiped as Kean, Lawrence and Northcote, Wilkie and Mulready, what space did they fill in the public eye compared with Young, Charles Kemble, or Macready?[2] Surely this renown is ample?

On Actors and the Art of Acting (Leipzig: B. Tauchnitz, 1875), pp. 57–60.

[2] Painters: Sir Thomas Lawrence (1769–1830), James Northcote (1746–1831), Sir David Wilkie (1785–1841), William Mulready (1786–1863); Actors: Charles Mayne Young (1777–1856), Charles Kemble (1775–1854).

On Natural Acting

It has commonly been held to be a dexterous and delicate compliment to Garrick's acting that Fielding has paid through the humorous criticism of Partridge, who saw nothing admirable in "the terror of the little man," but thought the actor who played the king was deserving of great praise. "He speaks all his words distinctly, half as loud again as the other. Anybody may see he is an actor." I cannot say what truth there was in Partridge's appreciation of Garrick, but if his language is to be interpreted as Fielding seems to imply, the intended compliment is a sarcasm. Partridge says, with a contemptuous sneer, "He the best player! Why, I could act as well as he myself. I am sure if I had seen a ghost, I should have looked in the very same manner, and done just as he did."[1]

Now assuming this to be tolerably near the truth, it implies that Garrick's acting was what is called "natural"; but *not* the natural presentation of a Hamlet. The melancholy, sceptical prince in the presence of his father's ghost must have felt a tremulous and solemn awe, but cannot have felt the vulgar terror of a vulgar nature; yet Partridge says, "If that little man upon the stage is not frightened, I never saw any man frightened in my life." The manner of a frightened Partridge can never have been at all like the manner of Hamlet. * * *

It is obvious that the naturalness required from Hamlet is very different from the naturalness of a Partridge; and Fielding made a great mistake in assimilating the representation of Garrick to the nature of a serving-man. We are not necessarily to believe that Garrick made this mistake; but on the showing of his eulogist he fell into an error quite as reprehensible as the

[1] Henry Fielding, *Tom Jones* (New York: Random House, 1940), pp. 758–761. Partridge is, of course, referring to the acting of the great David Garrick (1717–1779).

error of the actor who played the king, and whose stilted declamation was recognized by Partridge as something like acting.
That player had at least a sense of the *optique du théâtre* which
demanded a more elevated style than would have suited the
familiarity of daily intercourse. He knew he was there to act, to
represent a king, to impress an idealized image on the spectator's
mind, and he could not succeed by the naturalness of his own
manner. That he failed in his attempt proves that he was an
imperfect artist; but the attempt was an attempt at art. Garrick
(assuming the accuracy of Fielding's description) failed no less
egregiously, though in a different way. He was afraid of being
stilted, and he relapsed into vulgarity. He tried to be natural,
without duly considering the kind of nature that was to be represented. The supreme difficulty of an actor is to represent ideal
character with such truthfulness that it shall affect us as real,
not to drag down ideal character to the vulgar level. His art is
one of representation, not of illusion. He has to use natural
expressions, but he must sublimate them; the symbols must be
such as we can sympathetically interpret, and for this purpose
they must be the expressions of real human feeling; but just as
the language is poetry, or choice prose, purified from the hesi-
tancies, incoherences, and imperfections of careless daily speech,
so must his utterance be measured, musical, and incisive—his
manner typical and pictorial. If the language depart too widely
from the logic of passion and truthfulness, we call it bombast;
if the elevation of the actor's style be not sustained by natural
feeling, we call it mouthing and rant; and if the language fall
below the passion we call it prosaic and flat; as we call the actor
tame if he cannot present the character so as to interest us. The
most general error of authors, and of actors, is turgidity rather
than flatness. The striving to be effective easily leads into the
error of exaggeration. But it by no means follows, as some persons seem to imply, that, because exaggeration is a fault, tame-
ness is a merit. Exaggeration is a fault because it is an untruth;
but in art it is as easy to be untrue by falling below as by rising
above naturalness. * * *

If we once understand that naturalness in acting means truthful presentation of the character indicated by the author, and not the foisting of commonplace manner on the stage, there will be a ready recognition of each artist's skill, whether he represent the naturalness of a Falstaff, or the naturalness of a Sir Peter Teazle, or the naturalness of a Hamlet, or the naturalness of Coriolanus. Kean in Shylock was natural; Bouffé in Père Grandet. Rachel in Phèdre was natural; Farren in Grandfather Whitehead. Keeley in Waddilove was natural; Charles Mathews in Affable Hawk, and Got in Maître Guérin.[2] Naturalness being truthfulness, it is obvious that a coat-and-waistcoat realism demands a manner, delivery, and gesture wholly unlike the poetic realism of tragedy and comedy; and it has been the great mistake of actors that they have too often brought with them into the drama of ordinary life the style they have been accustomed to in the drama of ideal life.

On Actors and the Art of Acting (Leipzig: B. Tauchnitz, 1875), pp. 119–125.

---

[2] Marie Bouffé (1800–1888), famous comedian. See chaps. V, VI, VIII, XII of *On Actors and the Art of Acting*, for Lewes' descriptions of actors Farren, Keeley, Mathews, and Got.

Macready's Shylock

Perhaps of all Shakespeare's leading characters, Shylock[1] is the easiest of comprehension: drawn with firm bold strokes, it is more *scolpito* than the rest, and is not perplexed by the same involved complication of motives which renders Macbeth, Hamlet, Othello, Lear, and Leontes so easily misunderstood. Shylock stands as the representative of a persecuted race. Despised and hated by all around him, his religion scorned, his bargains thwarted, his losses mocked at, his friends set against him, his enemies heated, and all because he is a Jew! Even the mild and good Antonio—the pattern man of Venice—likened unto the best of ancient Romans—even he spits upon Shylock's gaberdine, and calls him "misbeliever, cut-throat dog." What is the consequence? Shylock, to hereditary hatred of the Christians, adds his own personal wrongs, and his malignity is the accumulation of years of outrage silently brooding in his soul. Much has he borne "with a patient shrug."

> For sufferance is the badge of all our tribe.

But as a Jew and as a man the incessant insults have made him lust for vengeance. Hence his exultant cry

> If I can catch him once upon the hip,
> I will *feed fat the ancient grudge* I bear him.[2]

He does catch Antonio on the hip. The man who hates the Jew's "sacred nation," and rails at him for his "usury," has fallen into his power; and so fierce, so relentless is his lust for vengeance that it conquers even his passion of avarice, and he refuses thrice the sum of his bond. Observe, in the great anguish of his heart

[1] Lewes played Shylock on March 10, 1849, at the Manchester Theater Royal, some twenty months before these comments appeared. He anticipated Sir Henry Irving in performing the role sympathetically.

[2] *Merchant of Venice*, I, iii.

at the loss of his daughter, the lost ducats hold an almost equal share; yet even his ducats he will lose rather than lose his vengeance on Antonio!

Nothing can, I think, be clearer than the malignity of Shakespeare's Jew, and its justification. We may perfectly acquit Shylock of being a "demon," though we admit the fierceness of his malignity. I put in this clause for a reason which will soon be apparent. I want to keep Shylock's human nature steadily in view.

Does Macready represent the Shylock of Shakespeare? To my apprehension not at all. It is a part in which even staunch thoroughgoing admirers do not applaud him; and the secret of his failure, I take it, lies in a radical misconception of the character; for assuredly so fine an actor could not be feeble in a part he truly seized. * * *

Macready's Shylock is an abject, sordid, irritable, argumentative Jew—not a haughty, passionate, and vindictive man whose vengeance is a retribution of wrongs to his sacred nation and to himself; and yet, although the devilish malignity has been suppressed, there is no restitution of the human affections in this Jewish bosom. Kean played Shylock as the personification of vindictiveness; yet in his ruthless bosom I always missed that affection for his child which even a malignant Jew must be supposed to have felt—in some degree, at least. But the absence in Macready's version is less excusable. Kean took what one may call the obvious view of Shylock, representing all that the plain *text* has given, and not troubling himself about anything lying *involved* in the text; hence, as Shakespeare gives no language of tenderness towards Jessica, Kean represented none. But Macready swerves from the obvious path—drops the ferocious malignity and lust for personal vengeance—yet never seems to have asked himself whether Shylock had the affections of his kind; accordingly, in the single scene with his daughter, he is harsh and irritable, when he might so truly and effectively have thrown in a touch of paternal tenderness. As I said before, we must not keep Shylock's humanity out of view.

Whatever he may be to his oppressors, the Christians, he is a man with a man's affections to his own tribe. He loves the memory of his lost Leah; he loves Jessica. Shakespeare has given the actor an exquisite passage wherein to indicate the husband's tenderness; and I believe that in the scene with Jessica an actor may effectively show paternal tenderness. It is true the actor must *read into* the scene that which is not expressly indicated; but precisely in such interpretations consists the actor's art. I have no hesitation in saying that to omit the paternal tenderness is to alter profoundly the tragic structure of the play; for observe, if Shylock is a savage, blood-thirsty wretch, the whole moral is lost; if his fierceness is *natural* to him, and not brought out by the wrongs of the Christians, all the noble philosophy of the piece is destroyed; and the only way of showing that his fierceness is that of retaliation is to show how to others he is *not* fierce.

It may be objected that when Shylock discovers her flight he raves as much about his ducats as his daughter, which does not speak of great affection on his part. But I do not wish to paint him as an idolizing father—I wish merely to show that he is not without fatherly affection, and even fond fathers might very well utter such fearful imprecations as those which escape Shylock ("I would my daughter were dead at my feet, the ducats in her coffin")[3] on discovering that their daughters had not only fled with lovers of a hated race, but added robbery to elopement. As a set off against these angry words, read the sorrowful exclamation in the fourth act, "These be the *Christian* husbands! I had a daughter: / Would any of the tribe of Barrabas / Had been her husband, rather than a Christian!"[4]

Further, the tragedy is heightened if we suppose Shylock to be fond of his child; for then the rebellion of "his own flesh and blood" comes with a tenfold bitterness. To be sure, this makes Jessica more odious; but she is odious; and—I dare to say it—Shakespeare has committed a serious blunder in art by the mode in which he has represented Jessica, when he might easily have

[3] *Ibid.*, III, ii. "Would she were hearsed at my foot and the ducats in her coffin."

[4] *Ibid.*, IV, i. This should read: "I have a daughter; Would any of the stock of Barrabas . . . ."

secured all he wanted by throwing more *truth* into the conception. That a Jewess should love a Christian, for him forsake her home, and abjure her religion, is conceivable; but it was for the poet to show how the overmastering passion of *love* conquered all the obstacles, how love conquered religion and filial affection, and made her sacrifice *everything* to her passion. Instead of this, Shakespeare has made her a heartless, frivolous girl, who robs her father, throws away her mother's turquoise for a monkey, speaks of her father in a tone as shocking as it is gratuitous. Were a modern poet so to outrage nature and art, no mercy would be shown him. But I have little doubt that many readers are indignant at my temerity in accusing Shakespeare of such gross errors!

To return, however, to the principal point, I say if Shylock be not represented as having the feelings of our kind, *The Merchant of Venice* becomes a brutal melodrama, not a great tragedy. It is therefore imperative on the actor that he seize every possible occasion to indicate these feelings. No Shylock that I have seen does this; but Macready above all ought to have done so; because his Shylock is less demoniac than the others.

The Leader, November 9, 1850, p. 787.

Rachel and Racine

Rachel[1] was the panther of the stage; with a panther's terrible beauty and undulating grace she moved and stood, glared and sprang. There always seemed something not human about her. She seemed made of different clay from her fellows—beautiful but not lovable. Those who never saw Edmund Kean may form a very good conception of him if they have ever seen Rachel. She was very much as a woman what he was as a man. If he was a lion, she was a panther.

Her range, like Kean's, was very limited, but her expression was perfect within that range. Scorn, triumph, rage, lust and merciless malignity she could represent in symbols of irresistible power; but she had little tenderness, no womanly caressing softness, no gaiety, no heartiness. She was so graceful and so powerful that her air of dignity was incomparable; but somehow you always felt in her presence an indefinable suggestion of latent wickedness. By the side of Pasta[2] she would have appeared like a beautiful devil beside a queenly woman; with more intellect, more incisive and impressive power, but with less soul, less diffusive and subduing influence.

In her early days nothing more exquisite could be heard than her elocution—it was musical and artistically graduated to the fluctuations of meaning. Her thrilling voice, flexible, penetrating, and grave, responded with the precision of a keyed instrument. Her thin, nervous frame vibrated with emotion. Her face, which would have been common, had it not been aflame with genius, was capable of intense expression. Her gestures were so fluent and graceful that merely to see her would have been a rare delight. The ideal tragedies of Racine, which ignorant Englishman call "cold," were, by her interpretation, shown to be instinct

---

[1] Elisa Rachel Felix (1820–1858).

[2] Guiditta Pasta (1798–1865), Italian singer.

with passion and dramatic effect. But this was only in her early days. Later in her career she grew careless; played her parts as if only in a hurry to get through them, flashing out now and then with tremendous power just to show what she could do. * * * In what I have to say of her, I shall speak only of her acting in its better days, for it is that to which memory naturally recurs.

The finest of her performances was of Phèdre. Nothing I have ever seen surpassed this picture of a soul torn by the conflicts of incestuous passion and struggling conscience; the unutterable mournfulness of her look and tone as she recognized the guilt of her desires, yet felt herself so possessed by them that escape was impossible, are things never to be forgotten. What a picture she was as she entered! You felt that she was wasting away under the fire within, that she was standing on the verge of the grave with pallid face, hot eyes, emaciated frame—an awful ghastly apparition. The slow deep mournful toning of her apostrophe to the sun, especially that close—

> Soleil! je te viens voir pour la derniere fois—

produced a thrill which vibrates still in memory. The whole of the opening scene, with one exception, was inexpressibly affecting and intensely true. As an ideal representation of real emotions, it belonged to the highest art. The remorseful lines—

> Graces au ciel, mes mains ne sont point criminelles:
> Plut aux dieux que mon coeur fut innocent comme elles—[3]

were charged with pathos. And how finely expressed was the hurrying horror with, as it were, a shiver between each phrase, transient yet vividly indicated, when she confessed her guilt. * * *[4]

In the second act, where Phèdre declares her passion to Hippolyte, Rachel was transcendent. She subtly contrived to indicate that her passion was a diseased passion, fiery and irresistible, yet odious to her and to him. She was marvellous in the abandonment to this onward-sweeping madness; her manner was fierce and rapid, as if the thoughts were crowding on her brain

[3] *Phèdre*, I, iii.
[4] *Ibid.*, II, v.

in tumult, and she dared not pause to consider them; and such was the amazing variety and compass of her expression that when she quitted the stage she left us quivering with an excitement comparable only to that produced by Kean in the third act of *Othello*. In the fourth act came the storm of rage, jealousy, and despair; it was lit up by wonderful flashes. Like Kean, she had a power of concentrating into a single phrase a world of intense feeling; and even Kean himself could not have surpassed the terrific exclamation—

Miserable! et je vis![5]

Whoever saw Rachel play Phèdre may be pardoned if he doubt whether he will ever see such acting again. * * *

Very noticeable it is that Rachel could not speak prose with even tolerable success; deprived of the music of verse, and missing its *ictus*, she seemed quite incapable of managing the easy cadences of colloquial prose. The subtle influence of rhythm seemed to penetrate her, and gave a movement and animation to her delivery which was altogether wanting in her declamation of prose. Hence, among other reasons, the failure of her attempts in modern drama. As Kean was only truly great in Shakespeare and Massinger, Rachel was only truly herself in Racine and Corneille.

On Actors and the Art of Acting (Leipzig: B. Tauchnitz, 1875), pp. 35–41.

---

[5] *Ibid.*, IV, vi.

VI.
THE RISE AND FALL OF THE DRAMA

Aeschylus, Sophocles, and Euripides

"Lofty and dignified," says Quintilian of Aeschylus, "grandiloquent, often to a fault, but frequently uncouth and inharmonius:"[1] an excellent judgment, every word hitting some characteristic, and that the right one. Modern critics have rarely been so just. They have either treated him with frivolous disdain for the faults pointed at in the second half of Quintilian's judgment, or with exaggerated admiration for the beauties mentioned in the first. The idea of his sublimity must be accepted with some qualification. He is more simple than sublime; more *naïf* than terrible. This simplicity is often sublime; but it is often, *t* to modern tastes at least, trivial. It is the rudeness and triviality of the infancy of art, often more interesting than the finest polish; but interesting as an indication of the condition of the human mind at that period, not as the perfection of art. * * * What Aristophanes says of the language of Aeschylus, that his words were wedged like one who rends timber, breathing with gigantic breath * * *[2] is very true; but too much stress has been laid on this quality, or, rather, too little has been laid on the other quality, equally characteristic, viz., his simplicity. The *Prometheus* which is the most sublime in subject, is extremely simple in treatment; it has a straightforwardness which, often descending to triviality, and sometimes to bad puning, is characteristic of all early poetry. The *Prometheus* has none of the Agamemnonian rant; and even in the *Agamemnon* there is considerable *naïveté* amidst the "high-crested" compounds and strained metaphors. That Aeschylus is often bombastic all the

[1] "Sublimis et gravis et grandiloquens saepe usque ad vitium, sed rudis in plerisque et incompositus." Quintilian, *Institutio Oratoria*, trans. H. E. Butler (4 vols.; Loeb Classical Library; Cambridge: Harvard University Press, 1953), IV, Bk. X, 38.

[2] "ῥήματα γομφοπαγῆ, πινακηδὸν ἀποβπῶν γηγενετ φυσήματι." *The Frogs*, ll. 824–825.

world knows; few seem aware that he is at times extremely simple, straightforward, and even trivial. M. Patin has properly insisted on this.[3] You have only to read a single play to perceive it. There is an error, however, almost as widely spread as the notion of his bombast, though ludicrously contradictory to it, and that is the profundity of his art.

To suppose Aeschylus a profound artist, is to suppose that he who invented the art also perfected it; a feat never yet performed by mortal man. * * * Many things which strike the modern reader as the result of genius, were, in truth, no more than stage necessities; and for them contemporaries had no admiration. Thus, to take an example, while Prometheus is being chained to the rock by Vulcan, Power, and Strength, he remains imperturbably silent. * * * It is not till left alone that he bursts forth into passionate complaints, calling on earth, air, and ocean, to behold his woes. This is sublime; no one doubts that it is sublime; yet it was no stroke of the poet's art. Either from some eurhythmic tendency in the construction of the plays, as Gruppe, and, after him, Bode maintain; or else, and more probably, from motives of economy with respect to the actors, as Geppert asserts,[4] certain it is, that more than *two speakers* were never together on the stage in the plays of Aeschylus, with a trivial exception in favour of Pylades, who, in the *Choëphorae*, says a few words. This fact is indubitable. The invention of the third actor is due, as Aristotle expressly tells us, to Sophocles. Aeschylus only used two. Scholars have been much puzzled to account for the distributions of the *Prometheus* into parts. In the first scene the protagonist would take the part of Power, the deuteragonist that of Vulcan. Prometheus therefore must be silent. Here the difficulty becomes inextricable; for how, if Prometheus be not one of the actors in the prologue, does he suddenly become one at the close, since he has not left the place where he was fixed to the rock? * * * At the opening of the

---

[3] Henri J. G. Patin, *Etudes sur les tragiques Grecs* (3 vols.; Paris, 1843).

[4] Otto Friedrich Gruppe, *Ariadne* (Berlin, 1834), p. 143; George Heinrich Bode, *Geschicte der hellenischen dichtkunst* (5 vols. in 3; Leipzig, 1838–1840), III, 233; Karl E. Geppert, *Die altgrieschische Buhne* (Leipzig, 1843), p. 58.

play four persons are on the stage; two only speak. Why Strength should be silent, no reason beyond stage necessities has been offered. Why is Prometheus silent? They who dwell upon the poet's art, declare that Prometheus is silent in contempt: he is too proud to answer the sarcasms of his foe; too proud even to accept the pity of his friend. But let those critics turn to verse 905, and the scene which there ensues. Mercury insults Prometheus, and the Titan is *not* silent. He rails in good set terms; defies Zeus, scorns his messenger, and shrieks with pain. If at any time his pride was needed, it was needed then; yet he is fluent— scurrilously so. Why? Simply because the *two actors* are together. The Titan, who was willing enough to express his pangs to the Oceanidae and Oceanus, and also to his enemy, when no third speaker is on the stage, could not answer either friend or foe, when the two speakers were present.

Mistakes, such as that combated above, must always be made so long as we continue to judge of antique works by modern standards. Whatever we see in Aeschylus that affects us as sublime, we naturally, but sometimes erroneously, suppose was meant to be sublime. * * * Aeschylus was a great poet, and created the Greek drama. He is, perhaps, worthy of as much admiration as Sophocles, but not on the same grounds. * * * Viewed with reference to their intrinsic merit, his plays hardly bear comparison with those of his wondrous rival. * * *

Euripides was a wonderful poet, and possessed in a rare degree the power of expression and the language of passion; but he was not a dramatist of the class of Sophocles and Shakespeare. * * * Passages of overpowering beauty and exquisite pathos, choruses running riot in luxuriant imagery, and situations of absorbing interest, are read with delight. But passages do not make a drama. * * * Sophocles not only bears inspection, but invites it, improves upon it. Incessant study does but explore new miracles of beauty, which had before been unobserved. The familiar knowledge of each part only makes the whole seem more stupendous. Euripides dazzles, Sophocles delights. In separate passages, in particular scenes, Euripides is, perhaps, finer than his great rival; but no single play will bear comparison with

the *Oedipus, Ajax, Philoctetes,* or *Antigone.* The scenes of Medea
with her children, of Phaedra with her nurse, of Iphigenia about
to die, of Alcestis parting from her husband and children, though
not quite free from his besetting sin of rhetoric, are certainly
very masterly, very wonderful; but the plays themselves are by
no means equal to them. The two most palpable defects in his
method are the "Prologue" and the "Deus ex Machina." By these
he abdicated all claim to the two great tasks of a dramatist, viz.,
evolution and *denouement.* Having evaded these difficulties, he
was enabled to throw all his strength into the middle portion,
the easiest; hence the power of his separate scenes. Every person
conversant with the structure of a drama, will readily admit that
evolution and *denouement* form almost the only difficulties. It is
easy to invent complex situations; but to make them naturally
evolve from byegone conditions, and afterwards naturally grow
to a point which shall complete the subject and be a real *denouement,* is what few men can accomplish. But to introduce, as
Euripides does, a god or hero who circumstantially narrates the
present state of affairs with a glance at the past; to bring forward
the characters while at the white heat of passion, allowing them
to rant, weep, and reason; and, having placed them in complex
situations, to introduce a god who announces the decrees of fate,
and *affixes* a termination to all the struggles and complexities,
instead of letting them work out their own natural, logical termination: this is not to write a drama, but to use the drama as
a stalking horse, under cover of which to shoot the arrows of
rhetoric and moral reasonings. Golden arrows, perhaps; but they
do not justify the stalking horse. The drama once used for such
purpose, never recovered its dignity.

Euripides is a rhetorician, not a dramatist. He speaks *for* his
characters, instead of letting them speak. That impersonality
which has been so much admired in Shakespeare and Goethe
(and not sufficiently recognized in Sophocles), which is the key-
stone of dramatic art, Euripides never exhibits. * * * Rhetoric
was the vice and luxury of the age in which Euripides lived.
* * * To make the worse appear the better reason, was not only
the practice of the Agora, but of the philosophers; from the

quibbling of lawyers to the sophisms of demagogues and teachers, the Athenian passed to the banquet where the guests were quibbling, or to the theatre where the mythic personages displayed their forensic art. The wisest philosophers, and the plainest citizens, were equally beset with this forensic passion. What are the works of Plato but displays of laborious quibbling? Truth, and to show the nothingness of the reigning philosophy, were, perhaps, the ulterior objects; but the means, were they not dangerous displays of gladiatorial ingenuity. * * *

Rhetoric being the darling vice, Euripides, who pandered to it, became the darling poet. * * * Aristophanes might laugh at him, for treating of familiar household matters; he might, with wonderful sarcasm, deny him the lyre * * * but the audience appreciated such verses and such pathos better than the profound art of Sophocles. Art is for the *élite*. Some portion of the genius which creates is indispensable to the mind that appreciates. Euripides wrote down to his audience, and they applauded. * * *

Aeschylus sketched grand outlines; Sophocles filled them up. Euripides frittered away his picture by exclusive attention to details. The first, painted demigods and their passions; the second, painted passionate men; he made the drama human. The third, degraded the drama by making it prosaic. It came into the hands of Euripides as a statue, cold, elaborate and ideal. He added warmth, but destroyed the ideality; he lifted it from its pedestal, and placed it in the market-place. * * * Aeschylus is grand and trivial; Sophocles passionate and majestical; Euripides passionate and familiar.

"The Rise and Fall of the European Drama," *Foreign Quarterly Review,* XXXV (1845), 305–326.

Characteristics of the Spanish Drama

The Spanish Drama, inasmuch as it is national, is distinguished from that of other nations by certain characteristics which I will here endeavour to bring into view.

A. W. Schlegel has pronounced the Spanish Drama to be the same in kind as the English.[1] They both belong to the "Romantic" Drama. I have an aversion to that word "romantic," employed as a cant of criticism; it is used to cover a multitude of inanities, and to excuse a thousand faults; but its irremediable defect is its want of precise meaning. I have tried in vain amongst German, French, and English writers to discover one who seemed to have any definite idea attached to the word, and have never been able to get at anything nearer than this,—viz., that Classic Art is Pagan Art, and Romantic Art is Christian Art; that consequently Racine and Alfieri, who adopt the Greek model, are to be judged according to the "classic principle," while Shakespeare, Calderón, and Schiller are to be judged according to the "romantic principle." So great a contempt of facts, and such substitution of verbiage for ideas, will be found in no other classification that has ever been adopted by sane men.

Although the Spanish Drama may be the same as the English, because both are Romantic, they are otherwise no more the same than an Englishman is a Spaniard because both are moderns. The resemblance is simply that of form. The two dramas are opposed in spirit, object, and construction. They unite only on the common ground of difference from the antique in disregarding the unities and in largely mingling the comic with the tragic. In these two points there is certain resemblance; but who does not see that such resemblances are purely formal, and too trivial to become a ground of classification?

[1] A. W. Schlegel, *A Course of Lectures on Dramatic Art and Literature*, trans. by John Black (2 vols.; London, 1815), II, 97–98.

I have long thought that the fundamental characteristic of the Southern mind is what the Germans call its *objectivity*; while that of the Northern mind is its *subjectivity*. * * * I use the word in no ill sense when I call the Italian nature *sensuous*; neither do I imply any superiority when I call the German *reflective*. As far as single words can express such complex things, I believe these two express the distinctive characteristic of the nations. Or I might call the former plastic and definite; the latter dreamy and vague. * * * The thoughts of the Italian grow quickly into passions; in the German, passions, when not highly excited, have an irresistible tendency to weave themselves into thoughts; so that while in the one all ideas stimulate to action; his tendency being to throw everything *out* of him; in the other, actions stimulate thoughts: his tendency being to connect all outward things with his inward life. * * *

If the plays of Lope de Vega and Calderón (to cite only the greatest names) be compared with those of Shakespeare, the distinction above noted between the southern and northern minds may become apparent. Calderón and Shakespeare are the opposite poles of intellectual action. The tendency of the Spaniard is to transform all thoughts into sensations; that of the Englishman to transform all sensations into thought. Cervantes, in his oft-quoted preface, has this remarkable passage: "I was the first to represent the *phantoms of the imagination and the hidden thoughts of the soul, by introducing figures of them upon the stage,* with the universal applause of the spectators."[2] Calderón has largely availed himself of it. Thus, in the *Purgatory of St. Patricius*, Ennio fights with a cavalier, but finds his strokes are wasted on the air; the cavalier slowly raises his casque and shows himself a skeleton. "Dost thou not know thyself?" the skeleton exclaims; "I am thy image: I am Ennio!" This is certainly an extreme case of objectivity. On the other hand, compare Hamlet when the Ghost appears. In Calderón, we have seen not only the spiritual become sensuous, but the personality of the man become

---

[2] Cervantes' Preface to the 1615 edition of his plays, published by Juan Villaroel.

an *object*. In Shakespeare, we see the reverse; we see an object, striking on the *sense*, converted into a *thought*. The Ghost, so palpable to Hamlet's sense, and not only to his, but to the sense of others; the Ghost, which stands as a distinct definitive object before him, in likeness of his father, he more than half believes to be a phantasm of the mind; thus reversing the objective process, and turning the sensuous into the spiritual. In the same way Macbeth resolves the Weird sisters into mental phantasms. These are strong illustrations of the tendency of the Spaniard towards making his thoughts become things, and that of the Englishman towards making things become thoughts. * * *

Instead of the *dramatic evolution of character and passion,* which is always the aim at least of an English poet, the Spaniard rarely attempts more than the *evolution of plot.* The events are not chosen to elicit the separate phases of the minds of the actors, but to carry on the intrigue of a complicated story. The passions called forth are those which have direct reference to the incident about to occur, or just occurred. Rage, jealousy, love, and hate are there; but with them no recurrence to early days; no slight touches which reveal preceding conditions of the mind and the affections; no involuntary demonstrations of qualities studiously guarded from the public gaze. These men "wear their hearts upon their sleeves,"—at least as much heart as they are supposed to possess. Their feelings are definite, distinct. We detect no half-feelings, no mixed motives, no interpenetration of the interests and prejudices, no gusts of passion sighing into tender recollections, and then roused again to fury, such as Shakespeare so wonderfully depicts. The *man,* in short, is not before you, but the *passion*: the passion is there, but not the passionate man. Nowhere throughout the Spanish drama can you find a character: everywhere personifications. There are certain stereotyped forms which serve for almost every play; they are differently called, but not differently made. If you remember any person in these dramas, it is by what he *did,* and not what he *felt*; because the difference is only in the actions, not in individualities.

This is not the way with Shakespeare. He has drawn accom-

plished, heartless, intellectual villains in Iago, Edmund, and
Richard III; he has drawn jealous, impetuous, passionate husbands in Leontes, Posthumus, and Othello; he has drawn
wronged, patient, loving wives in Hermione, Imogen, and Desdemona. Yet so various, so distinct are all these individualities,
in the midst of their generic resemblances, that the general
similarity is rarely detected, and the characters never for an
instant confounded. So with his endless fools. Folly of all shades
and antics, shapes itself into distinctive realities. Who ever mis-
took the braggart Paroles for the braggart Pistol, the conceited
Bottom for the puffed-up Malvolio, the acquiescent Snug for the
acquiescent Verges, the dotard Dogberry for the dotard Polonius?
—And who could ever distinguish one *gracioso* of the Spaniards
from another? Who remembers even their names?

The reader sees at once how necessary it is to bear in mind
the distinctive tendencies of the two nations when he compares
the plays of Calderón with those of Shakespeare. The aim of each
was different. The audience was different. The English poet
always sets before him the task of illustrating *character* and
passion. His story is the means whereby this is to take place; it is
consequently subordinate to the higher aim. The Spanish poet,
on the contrary, sets himself the task of representing an interesting and complicated story; and for that purpose uses characters
and passions as the means. The story is his principal aim. In the
English poet the story is fused by the passions, and moulded by
the characters. It also reacts on the characters and elicits the
passions. The two things—event and character—mutually elicit
each other. The Spanish poet never attempts this difficult achievement. He uses character as the instrument and plaything of the
story. His persons influence the story by what they *do*, but never
by what they *feel*. Examine Iago or Richard III, and it will be
apparent that these are not merely men who *do* villainous acts;
but that villainy is the tone and colour of their *minds*, affecting
all conclusions, distorting all judgments. Everything that is
beautiful or sacred is associated in their minds with what is
obscene and corrupt. Examine one of Calderón's villains—such
as Ennio—and it will be apparent that this villainy is so apart

and distinct from his mind, that it looks like feigning or insanity: it is not the man Ennio thinking, but Calderón thinking *for* him. In the high sense of the word, the Spanish poets are not dramatists, they are only ventriloquists.

The objective tendency is also observable in their poetry, which stands in similar opposition to our own. It is not the expression of dramatic feeling; it is not passion working from inwards; it is ventriloquism. In our dramatists, the poetry is impregnated with the passion. It produces often the most electric shock by the employment of familiar words. And it does this because expressing real passion, not the fanciful analogies of a mind at ease sporting with its images. * * * The Spanish poet disregards the truth for the sake of saying something fanciful or striking; he is occupied with fanciful analogies, not with imaginative truth.

I may notice here another peculiarity of this drama, which consists in the curious mixture of rapid incident and brief dialogue, with the most wearisome rhetorical speeches, of a length unparalleled in the annals of the drama. The Greeks indulge in long descriptions; so do the French; but the Spaniards distance them by hundreds of lines. Speeches of two or three hundred lines are constantly occurring in the very thick of the action; speeches filled with digressions of bombastic metaphors, and metaphysical *concetti*. While the reader is anxious to get a clue to the mystery of the plot, he has to wade through these terrible displays of rhetoric. Tedious as these are to us, "tedious exceedingly," they form to a Spanish audience a high treat. * * *

I have now arrived at the consideration of a characteristic of this drama which it is imperative on the student rightly to appreciate; and which will form for him an entertaining and highly important subject of investigation. I mean the objective morality and religion of the Spaniards. Morality was not with them a virtuous habit, a radical belief colouring all other beliefs, influencing all other ideas, mixing as it were with their very life's blood. It was a submission to rigidily defined principles, which were incarnate in the church, the throne, and the escutcheon. Religion, loyalty, honour, were the three restraining principles.

Conscience, in our meaning of the word, there was none; but, in its place, the Holy Inquisition, the Catholic Faith, and the Tribunal of Opinion: these were terrible in their vengeance, rigid in their decrees. All men knew what crimes were, and what their punishment. Both were definitive, objective.

Let this objective morality be thoroughly understood, for in Spanish history and Spanish art its influence is all important. The foreigner, if Protestant, is shocked to find in all the Spanish plays a frightful immorality; so it appears to him. In *La Devocion de la Cruz* by Calderón, the hero is a true Byronic ruffian, "linked with one virtue and a thousand crimes." By his own confession, his life has been a series of revolting crimes; he talks "as familiarly" of robberies, murders, and incest, as maidens do "of puppy dogs." But in the midst of all this villainy there is a virtue. He says that he has always steadfastly believed in God, and always raised a cross upon the graves of his victims (a practice common with southern banditti), and hopes in consequence of this steadfast faith—a faith no corruption of his soul could impair—that he shall obtain salvation. And he obtains it! In the *Purgatorio de San Patricio*, which the German critics have extolled for its profound religious philosophy, the same morality is observable. Ennio is a still more atrocious villain than he of the *Devotion to the Cross*, and with less apparent religion to excuse him. He boasts that

> Horrid crimes, theft, murder, sacrilege,
> Treason and perfidy—these are my boast
> And glory!

He recounts a few exploits which have distinguished him, such as the murder of an old Hidalgo and the abduction of the daughter; stabbing another Hidalgo in his nuptial chamber and carrying off his wife. He sought refuge in a convent, and seduced one of the nuns. This apex of his villainy revealed to him the existence of his only virtue. He has a virtue, and one powerful enough to cover his multitude of sins. His seduction of the nun stung him with remorse, the first pangs of conscience he had ever felt. This glimpse of the true faith saves him. This terror of the offended church and tribute to her awful power is the cause of his salvation.

Similarly also, in *El Condenado por desconfiado*, by Tirso de Molina, there is a hermit whose life has been a life of virtue, stained and distorted by one unpardonable crime, that of religious doubt. He doubts the divine clemency; doubts whether he shall be saved. This damns him. His soul is precipitated into the abyss at the same moment that a bandit, who perishes on the scaffold for his crimes, dies penitent, and is saved!

To modern feelings—to Protestant opinions—this is very repulsive; and one might be tempted at first sight to regard it as a satire on the church, which thus unblushingly set at nought the claims of a virtuous career. But such an idea is banished on a moment's reflection. Calderón was not only a Spaniard and eminently religious; he was also a member of the Holy Inquisition, and was not one to tamper with its dogmas. The religious Spaniard would have no repugnance to such an apotheosis of faith. And we can understand M. Ochoa (Calderón's latest editor) when he says that the *Devotion to the Cross* contains *una idea altamente social*.[3] But we cannot understand how Protestants should be so carried away by the cant of criticism as to see anything like profound philosophy in it. * * *

A comparison of confession with remorse will further elucidate the present subject. The Catholic commits a sin. Having confessed—having thrown it out of him, and from him—the penance once undergone, he is again joyous and sinless. The Protestant has no such means of shaking off remorse; it is a terrible monitor within, perpetually reminding him of his transgression. Remorse has been admirably defined as an *anticipation of the opinion of others*.[4] Now in confession a man gets rid of this "perilous stuff which weighs upon the heart." He owns his transgression, and its enormity is measured by the penance imposed. The vague uncertainty of fear no longer haunts him. He knows

[3] M. Ochoa (ed.), *Tesoro del Teatro Español: Tomo Tercero Teatro Escogido de Calder de la Barca* (Paris, 1838), p. 69.

[4] Sir Henry Taylor, *The Statesman* (Cambridge, England: W. Heffer, 1927), p. 47.

the *extent* of his sin and of his punishment. With the Protestant how different! He cannot measure the enormity of his sin; he has no definite penance awarded; he cannot know the opinions formed of his action by others; and it is this uncertainty, this anticipative fear, which constitutes the horror of remorse. He sees palliations for his act, which he knows his fellow men will not appreciate. * * * Lastly and awfully, how will his transgression appear to his eternal Judge? This question the Protestant is unable to answer; and in his uncertainty lies the terror. This question the Catholic has answered for him by his priest, who, as the mediator between him and offended Heaven, measures the sin and inflicts the proper punishment.

The student of Spanish and Italian history will frequently be puzzled at the contradictions in character which this objectivity of the southern religion induces. He will often see the grossest moral laxity united to intense religious fervour. He will find consummate atrocity, and reckless indifference to all men's good opinion, accompanied by unshaken faith and punctual observance of all rituals. The very Borgia are devout, and sincerely so. * * * In one word, the objective tendency is seen in the idolatry of the form and indifference to the spirit: faith, not works; ritual, not feeling.

The Spanish Drama: Lope de Vega and Calderón (London: Charles Knight, 1846), pp. 99–115.

Shakespeare

It must have been remarked by every one that criticisms on Shakespeare have been generally vitiated by the application of arbitrary principles, drawn from the Greek and the French drama; or else, through want of comprehensiveness, have sunk to the mere consideration of isolated passages and particular topics: while almost all attempts at enlarged and philosophic criticism have been unsatisfactory, in consequence of the critic not having distinctly set before him the aim and purpose of the poet. Much of this has arisen from a misconception of the office of criticism. Critics are not the Legislators, but the Judges and Police of literature. They do not make laws—they interpret and try to enforce them. Everyone admits that there could have been no Aristotle till there had been a Homer; but this admission is not carried far enough: it does not recognize the fact that the appearance of every truly original poet may probably originate new laws—which will need a new Aristotle. For what really is the meaning of "Rules of Art"? Are rules anything absolute in themselves, and binding upon all generations—or, are they not rather the conclusions which from time to time experience appears to have warranted, with respect to the best methods of attaining the artist's aim?

Before anything, therefore, can be settled about the rules of an Art, the *object* of the Art must be first distinctly ascertained. In the case of Shakespeare we are not aware of any critic having borne this in mind throughout, with the completeness and correctness which the case requires. Shakespeare was a Dramatic poet; but of all the numerous disquisitions on his genius, there have been none which, properly speaking, treat his works as dramas. As a poet, as a thinker, and as a delineator of character he has been praised, and described with nice discrimination. But as a *dramatic* poet, as the writer of dramas, scarcely any one has descended from generalities to point out his characteristic excellence. It is certain, however, that plays are not to be judged simply as poems. The drama is a branch of art peculiar in itself, aiming at peculiar effects, and achieving its effect by peculiar means. A drama is poetry applied to the purposes of the stage: and many a poem which may be exquisite in the closet would be unendurable on the stage. Architecture is not more the application of symmetry to the purposes of habitation, than the drama is the application of poetry to the purposes of the theatre. And as in architecture, we cannot regard beauty irrespective of utility, so neither in a drama will mere poetry succeed.

What then is the first purpose of a dramatist—the very condition at least, under which he works? *To interest and amuse an audience.* Let no one exclaim against this as a prosaic or degrading supposition. Prosaic or not, the fact is undeniable: People do go to the theatre for amusement. Whatever higher aims the dramatic poet may have in view, unless he amuses and sustains attention, he has failed. This is vividly shadowed out in the Theatre Prolog to *Faust,* wherein the manager and the poet typify the two elements of a drama; popular amusement and poetic beauty. The *means* are passion, character, poetry, and story, so combined as to rivet the attention of an audience; and while rivetting their attention, stirring and exalting the soul by that "purgation of passions"[1] which belongs to art. For art is not *mere* amusement; but something which, *through,* amusement, leads us into higher regions, and calls finer faculties into play. The purpose of the dramatist is this: Appealing to the vulgar instincts of curiosity, appealing to our delight in sensuous impressions, appealing to that sympathy which man feels for man, he seeks, while fixing our attention, at the same time to fill our fancy with images of exquisite beauty, and leave in us the abiding influence of great thoughts and noble aspirations.

To disregard the Stage in treating of the art of Shakespeare, is as if a man were to point out the mechanism of a watch, without any reference to its powers of indicating time. He may call upon us to admire the ingenuity and complexity of its mech-

---

[1] "παθημάτων κάθαρσις," Aristotle's *Poetics*, chap. VI.

anism * * * but after all we ask, does it keep time? Though it should be studded with diamonds, still it is a bad watch if it does not keep time. So with a drama. It may be poetical, it may have nice discrimination of character, it may be bright with gems —but it is a bad play if it fail to amuse an audience. Amusement is the preliminary condition; if that fail all fails. Vainly may critics agree on the merits of a tragedy, on its truth, its originality, its "correctness" according to the rules; if not a heart beats, if not an eye is wet with tears, the audience, in shameless defiance of Aristotle, will be cold—perhaps will yawn. Academies may lay down rules, but they cannot sway audiences; no audience ever wept academic tears.

It is not difficult to write rounded periods about the aim of tragedy being the purification of the passions, and about the stage being a secular pulpit from which great poets have delivered their lessons to mankind. But let us be frank. A direct question demands a direct answer. Did you ever in the whole course of your life "book two front seats in the boxes," or shield your wife from the crush at the pit door, under the impression that your passions were to be purified, and next Sunday's sermon anticipated? Did you not, on the contrary, book those places under the reasonable expectation of being amused—of having your eye dazzled by splendid scenery, your ear caressed by harmonious verse, your heart moved by the exhibition of passion? If you had not been amused, would you not have hissed? Moreover, remembering Shakespeare's position—at once the poet and the manager of a company—ask yourself this other question: What did Shakespeare think of, when he sat down to write a play? You will answer if you answer honestly,—"To fill the Globe theatre:" and you know he could only fill it by amusing the public.

To obviate misconception, we may distinguish here between *theatrical* and *dramatic* excellence, for we are by no means desirous of reducing Shakespeare to the level of a mere playwright. Amusement, we have said, is primarily sought at the theatre. Now, there being low amusements as well as refined amusements, and the lower faculties being more universally energetic in man

than the higher faculties, it is natural that the theater should be
furnished with plays which have no value beyond that derived
from acting. A good acting play may be a miserable poem; a fine
poem may be a miserable acting play; the art of the dramatist is
to unite the acting qualities of the one to the more refined and
enduring qualities of the other. * * * None of the powers which
we most admire may be necessary to produce a good acting play.
But, in proportion to the refinement of the subject, the difficulty
of combining theatrical excellence with poetic treatment becomes
greater,—so great indeed, that success in it is among the rarest of
literary triumphs. An ordinary man can model a rude figure out
of clay; but to bend the marble to the slightest caprices of the
mind, to make its stubborn material plastic to the most airy and
delicate conceptions, is the work only of a great artist. To take
an example from the dramatic representation of Character: However much we may delight in delineations of character for their
own sake, it must be remembered that the *art of the dramatist*
is not shown in the mere portrayal of mental states, but in the
adaptation of those mental states to *the purposes of the drama.*
A character may be drawn with skill, and yet not be dramatic.
All the traits which do not assist the fuller comprehension of the
story are superfluous and inartistic. Suppose jealousy be the passion of the play, as in *Othello.* For simple theatrical purposes the
writer may confine himself almost exclusively to this passion, and
only exhibit in Othello the jealous husband. It is obvious, however, that our sympathies will not be greatly stirred, unless in this
jealous husband we recognize other passions and other traits of
human nature; and the great problem is, so to contrive and combine these additional features, as not only to make the character
individual and engaging, but to help forward the action and
interest of the piece. An ordinary Moor in a paroxysm of jealousy
would be a far less touching sight than that of the highminded,
chivalric, open, affectionate Othello. The art of the *poet* is therefore to delineate these other qualities; and the art of the *dramatist* is to make them *dramatic agents* in the development of his
story. Accordingly, all that we see and hear of Othello are not
simply preparations for the exhibition of his jealousy and wrath,

but are circumstances skillfully adapted for bringing out the story. We thus learn both how the gentle Desdemona was justified in her love, and how Iago found him so easy a victim; so that at last we listen not only with patience, but compassion, to the noble speech, in which at the moment of executing his stern sentence on himself, he seeks to show that he was worthy of a better fate. Had Shakespeare introduced traits into this portrait which, though consistent in themselves, yet had no bearing on the general picture, he would have ruined its dramatic interest. People do not go to the theatre to learn Moorish customs or to analyse character, but to see a drama; and a drama is not a mirror of life in all its fulness and in all its details.—It is an episode in life, and must so be circumscribed.

These introductory observations bring to a point the debated question of Shakespeare's dramatic art, and place it in some degree in a new light. That he is the greatest of our Poets is an undisputed proposition—that he is the greatest of our Dramatists has also always been admitted; yet by a strange misconception he was long accused of "wanting art!" * * * In case his critics had been asked *what* art he wanted, they would unanimously have declared it was the art which they admired in the classics. Superior to the classics in the *effect* which he produced, he was supposed to be inferior in the *means!*

But unless the highest dramatic effects can be supposed to be the result of mere chance, they must have been the result of art. That "fluent Shakespeare scarce effaced a line,"[2] certainly was not true. To talk of "nature" and "inspiration" is easy enough; but whoever looks closely into these plays, noting their numerous failures and their numberless successes, will see at once that Shakespeare was a very careful, though perhaps not a theoretical artist. Instead of blinding himself over antique books, he closely watched the tempers of mankind; his rules were not drawn from ancient precedents, but from his own keen sense of the mode in which an audience was to be moved. What were the unities, what was the chorus, to him, who as manager, actor, and dramatist,

[2] Alexander Pope's "First Epistle of the Second Book of Horace," l. 279.

felt the living pulse of the public from day to day? How well, how nicely he discriminated the beatings of that pulse, his unparalleled successes have proved. Let us add that much of what amused an audience in *his* days—"conceits which clownage kept in pay"—and long poetical descriptions, will not amuse them *now*; hence the heaviness of some of his scenes on the modern stage. This change modern critics and dramatists too frequently overlook. They fall into the very error which they applaud Shakespeare for having avoided. They treat him as a classic—as a model to be slavishly imitated; until his genius has ended by consecrating as beauties the very defects which a wiser homage would have admitted to be blemishes,—spots on the sun, it is true, but still spots.

In his own day Shakespeare's triumph was complete. Even with his learned contemporaries, he had but one fault,—and that was a departure from classic models. From these models, Beaumont and Fletcher, who approached the nearest in popularity, departed as widely as himself. Then came the influence of French taste, which backed its pretensions not only by classic models, but by the masterpieces of Corneille and Racine. In spite of this taste, Shakespeare continued to hold undisputed sway over the hearts of Englishmen. No system of criticism could obscure the splendour of his genius. It was necessary, therefore, that an attempt of some kind should be made to reconcile the contradiction presented by a great poet, acknowledged to surpass the most finished artists in his effect, yet supposed all the time "totally ignorant of art." The reconciliation was brought about by means of the word "inspiration." In this attempt we read the idolatry of Shakespeare's admirers. Homer, indeed, might occasionally nod; Aeschylus be obscure; Euripides prosaic, and Virgil verbose and tautologous; for they were men.—But Shakespeare could have made mistakes only because he had not read certain classic authors: a tincture of learning would have infallibly guarded him from every error! If he wrote trash sometimes, it was to please the groundlings; while his false metaphors, disgusting images, and tedious speeches must have been "foisted in by the players." Thus Pope, in his celebrated Preface, attributed the bombast and triviality to be found in Shakespeare, wholly to the necessity of addressing a vulgar audience. * * *

We are afraid, however, that, from an infirmity of the human mind of which there are numerous examples, Shakespeare very sincerely admired those bombastic passages, and thought them truly grand; and that he probably had the same affection for his buffoonery and conceits as inveterate punsters have for their puns. An ingenious article on "Critical Induction" in the last number of the *Classical Museum*,[3] exposes the rashness of emendations which proceed upon no better ground than the improbability of eminent authors writing anything bad. Faultlessness is one of the privileges of mediocrity. It is with great geniuses, Longinus says, as with great riches:—something always must be overlooked.[4] Nor only overlooked: there will be even something in excess. We readily admit, therefore, that Shakespeare himself, were he alive, would be exceedingly amused at our making any difficulty in acknowledging his inequalities, and at our being at so much trouble to account for them, where they cannot be explained away.

"Shakespeare's Critics: English and Foreign," *Edinburgh Review*, XC (1849), 40–47.

---

[3] C. B., "Critical Introduction," *Classical Museum*, VII (1849), 2.

[4] Longinus, *On the Sublime*, trans. W. R. Roberts (2nd ed.; Cambridge: Cambridge University Press, 1907), p. 127.

On the Decline of the Drama (1850)

Light the fagots! Clear your throats for execration! Ransack your memory for epithets like stones to cast at our heretical heads! We are about to utter heresy of so black a dye that it will take the breath from some of you! It is nothing less than a conviction that the *greatest injury yet sustained by the English drama was the revival of admiration for the Old English Dramatists.* They were forgotten—justly so—

Nothing perishes but it deserves to perish.—Goethe[1]

forgotten in spite of their marvellous passages and lines of beauty, until Charles Lamb and his friends, struck with the brilliancy of the jewels cast upon these dunghills, cried out with all the quick delight of discoverers, "Here is a new world!" The old English dramatists were exhumed from the dust of oblivious ages, and were studied by our poets as models. Now we venture to say that more detestable models were never held up before a student's reverence; their very excellences being fatal lures. This is not the occasion for a survey of their characteristics, or a display of their peculiar infelicity as dramatists; but whoever has more than a second-hand acquaintance with Kyd, Peele, Marlowe, Webster, Dekker, Ford, Marston, Chapman, Heywood, Middleton, Shirley, Cyril Tourneur, and the rest, will probably agree with us that their plays are as poor in construction (artistic as well as theatric) as they are resplendent in imagery and weighty lines—that their characters are *sketched* rather than *developed*—that their situations for the most part are violent, horrible, and clumsily prepared, and that, besides being wearisome in reading, they are essentially unfit for the modern stage. If this be so—or

[1] *Faust*, Pt. I, ll. 1339–1340. "Den alles was entsteht/ Ist werth dass es zu grande geht." Everything that is born [or originates] deserves to perish. See G. H. Lewes' comment in *The Leader*, November 30, 1850, p. 859. "*The Duchess of Malfi* is a nightmare, not a tragedy."

but partially so—it follows that they cannot be good models for our living dramatists. The drama should be a reflex of our life, idealized, of course, but issuing out of the atmosphere we breathe. It *was* so when these writers lived: it was so in the reigns of Charles and Anne; it was so in the last century, when the British tar and British merchant were the claptraps of the stage. These last century tragedies and comedies are wearisome enough, 'tis true, and any escape from them might, to our young poets, have seemed an issue into a freer, healthier world. But the escape into the Old Drama was a brilliant fallacy: it was the Young Englandism of Art:[2] disgusted with the Present, yet without faith in the Future, it flew into the Past. Unhappily all our poets could learn in that Old Drama was precisely that of which (if they were poets) they stood in least need, viz., poetry; finding *that* there, they learned to think that poetry was enough to make a drama! Whereas, if they had never known this Old Drama, they must perforce have created a new form, and instead of the thousand-and-one imitations of the old dramatists, which the last twenty years have produced, we might have had some sterling plays. * * * To appeal to the public taste, to move the general heart of men, you must quit the study, and try to image forth some reflex of the world that all men know, speaking their language, uttering their thoughts, espousing their idealisms. Racine has been blamed by short-sighted critics for making his Greeks speak like Frenchmen: he did so because he was a *poet*, not an antiquary! Had he pictured Greeks (and how easy for one so learned to have done so!) he would have committed the mistake of our modern dramatists, viz., sacrificed the present to the past. We foresee an objection drawn from the continued success of Shakespeare and Racine; and we will answer it. Not *because* of their form—of what is temporal and peculiar to their epochs in them—do these masters hold us in their spell, but *in spite of it*. If they were born into this century they would not adopt the tone of two centuries past, but do now what they did then—reflect their

---

[2] A political movement, instigated by young Tories in 1842, which attempted to revive strong class distinctions. See *Coningsby* by Benjamin Disraeli.

age. This remark will also anticipate any question as to whether we wish *drawing-room* and *cottage life* to be the only sphere for a modern dramatist. We do not wish it. There is no need of abjuring the picturesque adjuncts of dress, scene, and distant time. Poetry moves more freely in a world of beauty and magnificence. But we do wish that the dramatist should not be an archaeologist, that he should not strive to revive defunct forms, but produce a nineteenth century drama: something that will appeal to a wider audience than that of a few critics and black-letter students. What has prevented our poets from attempting this? A preconceived notion of the excellence of the old English Dramatists!

The Leader, August 3, 1850, p. 451.

On the Decline of the Drama (1867)

In all countries and in all ages a really fine play must be a rarity, since it is a work which of all others demands the greatest combination of powers. It is not enough for a man to be a great poet, a great inventor, a great humourist—it is not enough for him to have insight into character, and power of representing it in action—it is not enough for him to have command over brilliant dialogue and striking situation—there must also be added to these, a peculiar instinct for dramatic evolution, a peculiar art of construction and ordonnance, which will combine all these qualities so as to meet psychological and theatrical exigencies. To be able to invent a story is one thing; to tell it dramatically is another; and to throw that story into the form of a drama is a third, and still more difficult, achievement. The poet who will keep his readers suspended upon his words, exciting their interest and sustaining it for hours, may not be able to move or amuse a theatrical audience during one short hour. Scott, for example, has few rivals in the art of telling a story, still fewer in the dramatic power of conceiving and representing character; yet no sooner did he attempt the drama than all his powers seemed paralysed; and, what is more, even his most dramatic novels have not made good dramas.

The drama is not merely poetry or literature; it is an *applied form* of these. A man may be a first-rate mathematician, yet wholly incompetent to an engineer's work; in like manner he may be a magnificent poet, yet an incompetent dramatist. Of this, poets are for the most part ignorant. They imagine that it will suffice if they throw a poetical story into dialogue, and divide it into acts and scenes. If it then *reads* beautifully, they conceive that it will *act* effectively. If the language is elevated and rich in images, the characters well devised and well drawn, the story interesting, what more remains for success? Let such a work be performed, and the exasperating indifference of the public will disclose some essential weakness in it; and any competent critic will be able to point out the source of that weakness. The work will be a poem in dialogue, not a drama to be acted. * * *

Very naturally the decline of the drama has been associated with the decline of good acting, and the paucity of good actors. Yet the fact is that at the time when our stage was in its most flourishing condition, the drama was pitiably poor. The greatest actors we have ever had—Garrick and Kean—failed to produce one single play of any permanent worth. And I am forced to recur to the old position, that the *chief* reason why we have not a brilliant dramatic literature is simply because we have not abundant dramatic genius.

Not that the causes which operate against the general cultivation of the theatre are to be set aside as of little account. They are real causes; and they are causes which no rhetoric or exhortation will enfeeble. Men will not change their habits in order to rescue an amusement from falling into utter neglect; and however preposterous may be the bigotry which condemns theatrical amusements, there is little chance of the self-styled "religious world" being taught either charity or sense, by its opponents. There is no difficulty in making any candid mind fully aware of the odious tyranny exercised by this "religious world" over the respectable classes, especially in the provinces; but unhappily the candid minds are rare in this body, and therefore you cannot get a hearing. It is in vain for you to argue that dancing is not sinful, that concerts are not sinful, that the pit of a theatre is no pit of perdition: the "religious world" sourly declares these things *are* sinful, and will never hear your protest to the contrary; or, hearing it, will declare that it leads to "scoffing unbelief." In England, whatever the "religious world" objects to, is apt to be branded as "leading to Atheism." Religious people outside the "religious world" are more charitable.

When it is said that the "religious world" has been increasing in its hostility to the drama, and that the general public has been growing more and more indifferent to it, enough has been said to explain the inevitable decadence. One gloomy section bitterly declaims against it because it is an Amusement (and all amusement beyond the control of the priest is sinful); the other section turns away from it because it is no longer amusing. And I think this second cause the more powerful of the two; for so strong is the natural desire for amusement, that even the "religious world" will seize any flimsy subterfuge to enjoy it. Thus, people who shudder at the idea of a theatre, crowd to see an actor or actress giving a dramatic representation in a concert room; and the pale-faced clergy, with their atrabiliar followers, who would consider a visit to the opera a step on the path of perdition, may be seen in great numbers listening to operatic singers and operatic music, provided they listen to it in Exeter Hall, or a provincial cathedral. Oratorios are mainly supported by this class. Yet were any dramatist daring enough to make a musical drama out of the Bible Histories—to place Saul, Elijah, St. Paul, or Eli on the *stage*, with dresses and decorations, every pulpit in England would resound with yells of execration at such a profanation. But Saul in a black coat and white waistcoat, singing with unmistakable operatic graces to a Michal in crinoline and flounces, is considered very edifying, if the musical drama be called an oratorio, and be performed out of a theatre!

Nor let it be argued that the "religious world" objects to theatres because theatres are centres of profligacy and vice; because things are said on the stage, and are seen off the stage, which propriety and morality severely disapprove. There was a time when such accusations were just—and that was a time when theatres flourished, and the drama occupied a considerable place in men's thoughts. It is no longer true of our theatres; they have been purified of these causes of offense—and the drama is rapidly decaying.

Lewes' edition of *Selections from the Modern British Dramatists* (2 vols.; Leipzig, F. A. Brockhaus, 1867) I, 6–12.

Selected Bibliography

Lewes' own list of his publications is to be found in his *Literary Receipts Book* (see below). The following is a list of some of his important books and articles. The articles are supplementary to those mentioned in the text.

A Biographical History of Philosophy. 4 vols. in 2. London: Charles Knight, 1845, 1846. Rev. ed. London: John W. Parker, 1857. Fourth ed. entitled *The History of Philosophy from Thales to Comte.* 2 vols. London: Longmans, Green, 1871.

Dramatic Essays, John Forster, George Henry Lewes, edd. William Archer and Robert W. Lowe. London: Walter Scott, 1896.

Literary Receipts Book. (Vol. VII in *The George Eliot Letters,* ed. Gordon S. Haight. 7 vols.) New Haven: Yale University Press, 1954–1956.

On Actors and the Art of Acting. Leipzig: B. Tauchnitz, 1875.

Problems of Life and Mind. 5 vols. London: H. Trübner, 1874–1879. First Series. *Foundations of a Creed.* 2 vols. 1874, 1875. Second Series. *The Physical Basis of Mind.* 1877. Third Series. *The Study of Psychology.* 1879. *Mind as a Function of the Organism.* 1879.

The Life of Goethe. 3rd ed. London: Smith, Elder, 1875.

The Principles of Success in Literature. ed. F. N. Scott. 3rd ed. Boston: Allyn, Bacon, 1894.

The Spanish Drama: Lope de Vega and Calderón. London: Charles Knight, 1846.

"Alfieri and the Italian Drama," *British and Foreign Review,* XVII (1844), 357–390.

"Actors and Managers: The Regeneration of the Drama," *Westminster Review,* XXXVII (1842), 71–97.

"Browning," *British Quarterly Review,* VI (1847), 490–509.

151

"Criticism in Relation to Novels," *Fortnightly Review*, III (1865), 352–361.

"Currer Bell's *Shirley*," *Edinburgh Review*, XCI (1850), 153–173.

"Dramatic Reform: Classification of Theatres," *Edinburgh Review*, LXXVIII (1843), 382–401.

"Goldoni and Modern Italian Comedy," *Foreign and Colonial Quarterly Review*, VI (1845), 333–368.

"Lessing," *Edinburgh Review*, LXXXII (1845), 451–470.

"On the Dread and Dislike of Science," *Fortnightly Review*, XXIX (1878), 808–815.

"Professor Bibundtucker's Remains," *Monthly Magazine*, VII (1842), 148–152.

"Shakespeare in France," *Cornhill Magazine*, XI (1865), 33–51.

"The Antigone and its Critics," *Foreign Quarterly Review*, XXXV (1845), 56–73.

"The Condition of Authors in England, Germany, and France," *Fraser's Magazine*, XXXV (1847), 285–295.

"The Life and Works of Leopardi," *Fraser's Magazine*, XXXVIII (1848), 659–669.

"The Miseries of a Dramatic Author," *Cornhill Magazine*, VIII (1863), 498–512.

"The Roman Empire and its Poets," *Westminster Review*, XXXVIII (1842), 33–58.

"The State of Criticism in France," *British and Foreign Review*, XVI (1844), 327–362.

"Walter Savage Landor," *Lowe's Edinburgh Magazine* (1846), pp. 28–34.

There exists as yet no definitive biography of Lewes, and the only full-length study of his thought is an Italian work on his philosophy. The following may help to illuminate various aspects of his philosophic and critical thought.

BRETT, R. L. "George Henry Lewes: Dramatist, Novelist and Critic," *Essays and Studies*, XI (1958), 101–120.

ELLIS, HAVELOCK. Introduction, *The Life and Works of Goethe*. Everyman Edition. London and New York: Dent, 1908.

GARY, FRANKLIN. "Charlotte Brontë and George Henry Lewes," *PMLA*, LI (1936), 518–542.

GRASSI-BERTAZZI, G. *Esame Critico della Filosofia di George Henry Lewes.* Messina: Trimarchi, 1906.

GREENHUT, MORRIS. "George Henry Lewes and the Classical Tradition in English Criticism," *Review of English Studies.* XXIV (1948), 126–137.

———. "George Henry Lewes as a Critic of the Novel," *Studies in Philology*, XLV (1948), 491–511.

———. "G. H. Lewes' Criticism of the Drama," *PMLA*, LXIV (1949), 350–368.

HAIGHT, GORDON S. "Dickens and Lewes on Spontaneous Combustion," *Nineteenth Century Fiction*, X (June 1955), 53–63.

———. "Dickens and Lewes," *PMLA*, LXXI (1956), 166–179.

KAMINSKY, ALICE R. "George Eliot, George Henry Lewes, and the Novel," *PMLA*, LXX (1955), 907–1013.

KAMINSKY, JACK. "The Empirical Metaphysics of George Henry Lewes," *Journal of the History of Ideas*, XIII (1952), 314–332.

KITCHEL, ANNA T. *George Lewes and George Eliot: A Review of Records* (New York: John Day, 1933).

WARREN, HOWARD C. *A History of the Association Psychology.* New York: Charles Scribner's Son, 1921.

Index

155